The Power and Precision of God's Word

Joshua Rhoades

Published by Joshua Paul Rhoades, 2024.

THE POWER AND PRECISION OF GOD'S WORD

First edition. November 9, 2024.

Copyright © 2024 Joshua Rhoades.

ISBN: 979-8227749116

Written by Joshua Rhoades.

Also by Joshua Rhoades

Courage Under Fire: David's Stand On The Battlefield
Jonah's Journey: Voices Of Redemption And Lessons In Obedience
The Furnace Of Faith: 12 Principles From The Heat Of Faith
Whispers of Hope: Inspiring Stories of Men's Prayers In Scripture
Frontier Legends: The Oregon Dream
Elijah: A Beacon Of Boldness
HOOK, LINE & SAVIOUR - Faith Reflections from Fishing
Driven By Faith: Motor Racing Inspired Christian Life
30 Day Devotional - Bold and Strong- Coffee Devotions for a Courageous
Christian Walk
Authentic Christianity: The Heart of Old Time Religion
Consider The Ant - God's Tiny Preachers
Flee Fornication: The Plea For Purity
Renewed Hope- How to Find Encouragement in God
Sounding The Call - The Voice of Conviction
The Altar - Where Heaven Meets Earth
The Bible's Battlefields- Timeless Lessons from Ancient Wars
The Sacred Art of Silence - How Silence Speaks in Scripture
Under Fire- The Sanctity of the Traditional Biblical Home
Who Is on the Lord's Side? A Call to Righteousness
What Is Truth? - From Skepticism to Submission
First and Goal- Faith and Football Fundamentals
From Dugout to Devotion- Spiritual Lessons from Baseball
Par for the Course- Faith and Fairways
The Believer's Pace- Tools for Running Life's Marathon
The Immutable Fortress- Security in God's Unchanging Nature
Biblical Bravery
Deer Stands and Devotions: A Hunter's Walk with God

Jesus Knows- Our Hearts, Our Responsibility
Restoration - Setting The Bone
Spiritual 911- God's Word for Life's Emergency's
The Freedom of Forgiveness
The Jezebel Effect - Ancient Manipulations Modern Lessons
The Shout That Stopped The Saviour
The Time Machine Chronicles: Old Testament Characters
Anchored In Truth Exploring The Depths of Psalm 119
Biblical Counsel on Anger
Proverbs' Portraits The Men God Mentions
Stumbling in the Dark - The Dangers of Alcohol
Guarding the Wicket Protecting Your Faith and Game
The Champion's Faith - Wrestling and Achieving Spiritual Victory
Scriptural Commands for Modern Times Living God's Word Today Volume 1
Scriptural Commands for Modern Times Living God's Word Today Volume 2
Scriptural Commands for Modern Times Living God's Word TodayVolume3
The Greatest Gift
A Christmas Journey of Faith
Daughter Of The King: Embracing Your Identity In Christ
Determination and Dedication Building Strong Faith As A Young Man
Walking Through Walls God's Power to Part the Storms of Life
David's Song Of Deliverance Praising God Through Every Storm
From Weakness to Warrior: Gideon's Transformation
Why Did Jesus Weep?
Living For God The Call To Be A Living Sacrifice
My Mind Is In A Fog What Do I Do?
Turning The Page Written By Grace
The Calling and Greatness of John the Baptist
For Such a Time Esther's Courageous Stand
From Brokenness To Beauty Written By The Pen of Grace
The Ultimate Guide to Massive Action- From Plans to Reality
A Heart Of Conviction
Serving In The Shadows
Repentance Revealed The Road Back To God
The Chief Sinner Meets The Chief Saviour Reflections On I Timothy 1:15

Answer The Call - 31 Days of Biblical Action
The Birthmark of the Believer
Reflections on Calvary's Cross
The Kingdom Builder Paul's Bold Proclamation of Christ
The Animal Of Pride
The Reach That Restores Christ Love For The Broken
Paul- The Many Roles of a Servant of Christ
Unshakeable Faith- 31 Days of Peace in God's Word
O Come, Let Us Adore Him- A Christmas Devotional
The Shepherd's Voice
The Trail From Vision To Mission
Enabled- Living God's Purpose With Power
Held Back But Not Defeated
The Power and Precision of God's Word

Dedication

To you, the reader of "The Power and Precision of God's Word", this dedication is meant for you with deep sincerity and hope. You've come to these pages, drawn perhaps by a desire to grow, to understand, or to experience God's Word in a new way. Maybe life has challenged you in ways you didn't expect, or perhaps you feel called to dive deeper into God's promises, seeking comfort, guidance, and strength. Whatever brought you here, know this: you are seen, known, and cherished by God. He desires to meet you exactly where you are, offering His love, His wisdom, and His strength through the powerful words you'll encounter in these pages.

This book was created to remind you of the life-changing truth that God's Word is not only for others, but for you personally. His Word is alive and active, a light that can illuminate even the darkest moments and bring hope in the midst of confusion. This dedication is for you who may feel weary, carrying burdens that seem too heavy to bear. It's for those moments when life feels uncertain, when doubt creeps in, or when faith feels distant. May you find in God's Word an anchor for your soul, a steady and unwavering guide that reassures you of God's presence and His purpose for you.

As you journey through this book, my prayer is that each page draws you closer to God, opening your heart to the depth of His love and the precision of His promises. May you discover that God's Word is not just a collection of old stories or moral teachings but a living, breathing message meant to guide, comfort, and strengthen you right where you are. Each verse has the power to renew your mind, lift your spirit, and give you hope that endures even the toughest challenges.

For the times you feel uncertain or inadequate, remember that God's Word equips you with all you need to stand strong and walk confidently in faith. It speaks to every corner of your life, bringing light to areas that feel hidden or broken and inviting you to experience God's healing and peace. Embrace these pages with an open heart, allowing Scripture to reshape your perspectives, renew your hope, and ignite a deeper sense of purpose within you.

This book is dedicated to you—your journey, your growth, and your faith. May these words encourage you to hold onto God's promises, to live with courage and compassion, and to know, above all else, that you are deeply loved by a God who desires to speak directly to you through His Word. May this experience be more than just reading; may it be a transformative journey that brings you closer to the heart of God, reminding you of the unchanging truth that His Word is a powerful, precise, and personal gift meant just for you.

"God's Word is not just a collection of ancient writings; it is the living, words of Almighty God, that reaches into the depths of our souls, bringing clarity, comfort, and guidance for every part of our lives. It reveals God's heart, offers unshakeable truth, and calls us into a closer relationship with Him. Embracing the Bible means more than reading words on a page—it means allowing each verse to shape us, strengthen us, and speak to our deepest needs. "The Power and Precision of God's Word" invites us to experience Scripture as a constant companion, the source of wisdom, and the guide that helps us live with our faith, courage, and walk with the Lord."

Introduction

Welcome to "The Power and Precision of God's Word", a book that explores the incredible impact of the Bible on our lives. God's Word is not just a book of ancient stories or wise teachings; it's a living, powerful message with the ability to transform hearts, bring hope, and offer guidance for every situation we face. The Bible reveals who God is, shows us His love, and invites us into a deeper relationship with Him. For Christians, understanding the importance and capability of God's Word is essential because it provides the foundation of our faith and directs our steps. Each verse holds a truth that can touch and change our lives, if we allow it to. Whether we're dealing with confusion, searching for direction, or simply trying to live with purpose, Scripture has the answers we need. This book will show how God's Word penetrates deeply into our hearts, discerning our thoughts and intentions, and helping us grow spiritually, emotionally, and morally. It's designed to teach us not only to read the Bible but to truly understand its power—to realize that this is not just a historical text, but the voice of God speaking into our lives.

The Bible is unique in its ability to reach every aspect of who we are, guiding us to make wise decisions, strengthening us against temptation, and comforting us in times of sorrow. Through God's Word, we gain wisdom that helps us navigate challenges with confidence and clarity. It's a source of strength that reminds us we're never alone, that God's presence and promises are with us always. But the Bible's importance goes even deeper; it not only changes the way we live but transforms who we are, helping us to grow into the people God created us to be. This book will examine the "precision" of God's Word—its ability to reach specific areas of our lives, whether it's healing a broken heart, correcting a wrong path, or providing hope in what seems like a hopeless situation. As we explore these themes, we'll see that every page of Scripture is filled with intentional, powerful words meant to lead us closer to God and to show us how to live with faith, courage, and love.

Understanding the power of God's Word means realizing that we have access to God's wisdom, love, and guidance at all times. It's a gift that offers unchanging truth in a constantly changing world. This book will help readers discover how to lean on Scripture for strength, wisdom, and encouragement and see how God's promises apply to our everyday lives. It will challenge us to let Scripture not just be something we read, but something we live out, shaping our attitudes, words, and actions. The Bible equips us to face life's difficulties with hope and purpose and to experience peace even in the midst of challenges. By the end of this journey, we will come to see God's Word not as a set of rules or distant ideas, but as a guide and companion that gives us life, joy, and direction. "The Power and Precision of God's Word" invites us to embrace the Bible fully, to recognize its relevance, and to let it work within us, changing us from the inside out and drawing us closer to God each day.

Chapter 1 – Sharpness

"The Power and Precision of God's Word" is a beautiful concept that shows us how meaningful and life-changing God's Word truly is. When we say that God's Word is "sharper than any twoedged sword," it means that the Bible, the Scriptures, and God's messages to us are so powerful that they can penetrate deep into our hearts, minds, and souls. Just like a sharp sword cuts through materials easily and precisely, God's Word cuts through confusion, dishonesty, and anything that keeps us from understanding the truth. Think of a sword with two edges: it can cut in two directions. God's Word is similar, but even more powerful because it doesn't just cut; it clarifies, refines, and shapes us. When we read, listen to, or reflect on God's Word, it can reach the deepest parts of who we are, helping us see things clearly and encouraging us to live according to truth and righteousness.

Imagine trying to cut something with a dull blade. It's hard, right? You might push, slice, or saw away at it, but it takes a lot of effort, and the cut is usually not clean. Now, think about using a sharp knife or blade. With less force, you get a smooth, clean cut, and it doesn't take as much effort or strain. This is what it's like with God's Word. When we let God's Word sharpen our understanding, it helps us separate right from wrong, good from bad, and true from false. It's like a bright light in a dark room, showing us the way, exposing what's hidden, and helping us see things as they really are.

The precision of God's Word means it's exact and perfect for every situation in our lives. It's not vague or general; it speaks directly to our needs, thoughts, and circumstances. When we are uncertain, God's Word can give us wisdom. When we're afraid or anxious, it provides peace. When we struggle with temptation, it strengthens us to resist and follow what's right. In this way, the Bible is more than just words on a page; it is a tool, a guide, and a source of strength that can deeply impact our lives. It knows where to reach us and speaks to our innermost thoughts and desires. This is what it means to have precision: it doesn't just skim the surface; it goes straight to the heart of the matter, helping us to understand ourselves and God's plans for us better.

Allowing God's Word to refine and sharpen us means being open to change and growth. Sometimes, it's not easy to let the Bible point out areas in our lives that need improvement, but it's necessary for becoming a better person and follower of Christ. Just as sharpening a blade makes it more effective, letting God's Word sharpen our character, decisions, and attitudes makes us stronger and more faithful. When we read the Bible and let it guide us, it challenges us to look at our thoughts and actions honestly. Are we being truthful? Are we acting with love and kindness? Are we standing up for what's right? These questions become clear when we let God's Word work within us.

Bringing clarity to our faith is another wonderful effect of God's Word's sharpness and precision. Faith can sometimes feel confusing, especially when we face doubts or struggles. But the Bible cuts through this confusion, helping us understand who God is, who we are, and what we're called to do. By reading and studying Scripture, we gain confidence in our beliefs and trust in God's promises. It's like looking through a foggy window that suddenly becomes clear. We can see God's love, grace, and purpose more clearly, and our faith grows stronger.

In our daily lives, applying the sharpness of God's Word means letting it influence how we think, speak, and act. When faced with a tough decision, we can look to Scripture for guidance, trusting that it will help us choose wisely. When dealing with difficult people or situations, God's Word can remind us to be patient, kind, and forgiving. Each time we let God's Word sharpen our responses and actions, we reflect His love and truth to others, becoming more like Him in our words and deeds.

In conclusion, the sharpness of God's Word is a gift that helps us cut through life's challenges and stay grounded in truth. It has the power to shape us, correct us, and encourage us, making our faith clearer and stronger. When we open ourselves to its refining and sharpening work, we become more aligned with God's will, living lives that honor Him and reflect His love. Just as a sharp sword is a powerful tool, so is God's Word in the life of a believer. It equips us to face whatever comes our way, confident that we are guided by His perfect wisdom and love.

Chapter 2 - Spirit and Soul Distinction

The "Spirit and Soul Distinction" is a meaningful concept that reflects the unique power of God's Word to reach into the deepest parts of who we are, making clear distinctions within us that we might not fully understand on our own. When the Bible says that the Word divides "soul and spirit," it points to the ability of Scripture to reach beyond just the surface of our lives and go into the core of our being, identifying and separating things that may be tangled up inside us. In the Bible, the soul and spirit are two essential but different aspects of a person. The soul often represents our natural, human part – our thoughts, emotions, and desires that come from our earthly experiences. This part of us connects to what we feel, think, and want, and is heavily influenced by the world around us. The spirit, on the other hand, represents the part of us that connects directly with God, our capacity to understand spiritual truths, and our openness to God's influence and guidance. The spirit is where our relationship with God becomes alive, where we can sense His presence and hear His voice. This difference between soul and spirit can be hard to identify on our own because, in daily life, our feelings, thoughts, and desires can often seem mixed together, making it challenging to know what comes from our natural self (soul) and what comes from the divine guidance (spirit) that God provides.

God's Word has the unique power to separate these parts, helping us understand where our actions, thoughts, and decisions are being driven by worldly desires or by spiritual truths. The Bible acts like a spiritual mirror, reflecting back to us what is coming from our human desires and what is inspired by God's guidance. For example, we may feel strongly about something or have a certain goal we want to achieve, but through Scripture, we might realize that this desire is driven by selfish motives or worldly values. In contrast, there are desires and goals that arise from a place of love, kindness, and faith, aligning with God's will, which are rooted in the spirit. The Word of God allows us to examine these inner parts, giving us clarity to discern if we are pursuing something out of personal ambition or out of a genuine desire to follow God's path. When we dive into Scripture, it's like a light shining into our hearts, revealing where we need to align more closely with God's values. The Bible doesn't just give us rules; it speaks to us personally, addressing our specific needs and guiding us to make distinctions that lead to spiritual growth. By reading God's Word, we become better at recognizing what's influenced by temporary, earthly concerns and what's inspired by eternal, spiritual truths. This division is essential for a life of faith because it helps us prioritize and follow what truly matters, what brings us closer to God, and what serves His purpose.

The importance of distinguishing between soul and spirit becomes even clearer when we face difficult situations or big decisions. Often, our natural self, or soul, may feel one way—such as fearful, anxious, or doubtful—but our spirit, grounded in faith, points us toward trust and courage. For instance, we might feel tempted to make choices that prioritize our comfort or success, even if it means compromising on our values. However, through Scripture, we are reminded that God's ways are higher, urging us to follow His guidance rather than our immediate, earthly desires. This separation between soul and spirit is not always easy, but God's Word provides the wisdom to see beyond our initial reactions or emotions. It teaches us that true fulfillment doesn't come from following fleeting desires but from aligning our lives with spiritual truths that honor God. In this way, Scripture helps us see that our spirit seeks what is pure, lasting, and aligned with God's will, whereas the soul may lean toward temporary pleasures or worldly success. Understanding this distinction allows us to live a more intentional life, focusing on what truly brings peace and fulfillment, rather than being tossed around by every emotion or desire.

Seeking God's Word to help us understand the difference between fleshly desires and spiritual truths is a lifelong journey, but it's one that transforms our lives in profound ways. As we turn to Scripture daily, we develop a sharper sense of what God desires for us, and we begin to recognize how often our natural inclinations may conflict with His plan. The Bible shows us examples of people who followed their human desires and faced challenges, as well as those who followed God's guidance and found true peace. For example, characters in the

Bible like David, who at times followed his personal desires but then returned to God's path, teach us about the importance of distinguishing between soul-led and spirit-led choices. Each story and teaching in Scripture provides us with insight into the results of following either the soul or the spirit. This helps us understand the importance of aligning ourselves with the spirit, living by values of love, humility, and trust in God.

Applying this distinction in our daily lives also means we become more aware of our own intentions. Are we acting out of love, compassion, and a desire to serve, or are we being driven by pride, selfishness, or fear? The Bible doesn't only reveal these truths to us; it also empowers us to change. By following its guidance, we can move away from actions driven by the soul and focus on choices that strengthen our spirit. This application is essential in all areas of life, whether in our relationships, work, or personal goals. For example, in a disagreement with someone, our natural reaction might be to defend ourselves or prove a point, driven by pride or anger. But when we seek God's Word, we are reminded to act in kindness, patience, and forgiveness—values that stem from the spirit rather than the soul. Each time we choose to act based on spiritual truths, we grow closer to God and become more like Christ.

Ultimately, the power of God's Word in distinguishing between soul and spirit is a gift that allows us to live a life centered on His purpose and love. It's not about ignoring our natural desires but learning to discern and align them with God's will. When we do this, we experience a deeper sense of peace, direction, and fulfillment. By continually seeking the wisdom of Scripture, we gain the strength to make choices that honor God, transforming us from the inside out. This ongoing process of refinement helps us to live as God intended, with a heart focused on eternal truths and a life that reflects His love to those around us. Through God's Word, we are reminded that while our soul connects us to the world, our spirit connects us to God, and it's by following the spirit that we find true meaning and joy. Each time we read and apply the Bible, we are sharpening our ability to distinguish between these parts, growing stronger in faith and more connected to the purpose God has for us. This distinction isn't a one-time realization but a daily practice, one that leads to a richer, more faithful life that brings glory to God.

Chapter 3 - Surgical Precision

The concept of Surgical Precision in describing God's Word is about understanding how incredibly exact and focused it is in dealing with the deepest parts of who we are. When we read that God's Word "pierces even to the dividing asunder," it paints a picture of a powerful, sharp instrument that is able to reach places within us that no other tool can touch. Imagine a surgeon's scalpel, which has to be both incredibly sharp and carefully handled in order to perform surgery without causing unnecessary damage. The scalpel has a unique purpose—to carefully cut into the body, precisely and exactly where it is needed, to heal or remove something harmful. In a similar way, God's Word acts like a spiritual scalpel, able to penetrate deeply into our minds and hearts, cutting through layers that are sometimes thick with confusion, pride, fear, or self-deception. Just as a skilled surgeon would use a scalpel to open up and address what's going on beneath the surface, God uses His Word to expose and address the hidden thoughts, motives, and intentions we may not even realize we hold. This isn't a harsh or reckless kind of cutting; it is a careful, loving, and intentional action aimed at bringing healing, growth, and clarity to our lives.

One of the amazing things about the precision of God's Word is that it knows exactly where to reach us. Unlike human tools or advice that may only scratch the surface or offer temporary fixes, the Bible goes straight to the core issues in our hearts. It doesn't waste time or avoid uncomfortable truths. Instead, it speaks directly to the real problems, the hidden motives, and the unspoken fears that often lie buried beneath layers of daily life, habits, or past experiences. Sometimes, we may build up walls within ourselves, perhaps because we're afraid of facing certain truths or because we've been hurt in the past. These walls can block our growth and keep us from fully experiencing God's love and purpose for our lives. But when we allow God's Word to work within us, it's like a precise, focused tool that cuts through these barriers, revealing what's really going on inside us. This can be a challenging process because it requires us to confront things we might rather ignore, but it is also deeply freeing. God's Word doesn't cut us open to hurt us; it reveals what's necessary for us to grow and become whole. By addressing what is hidden and often ignored, the Word helps us to see ourselves more clearly and, ultimately, to understand and live out God's intentions for us.

The idea of the Word having this surgical precision also means that it's incredibly specific. It's not a one-size-fits-all approach; instead, it speaks to each person uniquely. Just as every medical surgery is tailored to the needs of the patient, the impact of God's Word is tailored to the individual needs, struggles, and situations of each person. What God's Word says to one person might be different from what it says to another, depending on where they are in life and what they need to hear. It has the power to convict one person of pride while encouraging another who feels defeated. It can challenge someone to let go of anger and, at the same time, give hope to another who feels lost. This precision is what makes God's Word so incredibly powerful and personal. It reaches us exactly where we are and speaks to the specific issues we face, cutting through the noise of the world and going straight to what matters most.

Letting God's Word address the hidden motives and deep-seated issues within our hearts is not always easy, but it's one of the most valuable things we can do in our spiritual journey. Hidden motives are those reasons or intentions behind our actions that we may not be fully aware of or willing to admit. For example, someone might do good deeds but, deep down, is motivated by a desire for praise or recognition rather than genuine kindness. Others may seek success, thinking it's for a good cause, but, upon closer examination, realize it's rooted in a need to prove themselves or feel superior. God's Word helps us see these motives clearly. It doesn't just look at what we do; it examines why we do it. By doing so, it allows us to align our intentions with God's will and helps us live a life of true integrity. This process can be uncomfortable because it reveals parts of us we might prefer to keep hidden, but it's also incredibly liberating. When we allow God's Word to confront these deep issues, we begin to let go of unhealthy patterns and habits that hold us back.

Furthermore, God's Word's ability to cut through layers means it addresses both the obvious and the hidden. We all have layers built up over time—layers of defense, layers of denial, and even layers of pain that we carry from past experiences. These layers can sometimes cloud our judgment, making it difficult to know what we truly need or how to respond to God. The Bible has the unique ability to peel back these layers, one by one, going beyond what is outwardly visible and revealing what lies beneath. Sometimes we might think that we have forgiven someone or moved on from a hurtful experience, but, through Scripture, we may find that there are still unresolved feelings or thoughts holding us back. This deep work is not meant to make us feel ashamed or guilty; instead, it's a process that leads us toward healing. Just as a surgeon might need to make an incision to remove something harmful, God uses His Word to cut through what doesn't belong, freeing us from the things that weigh us down and prevent us from living fully in His love.

The precision of God's Word is also vital when it comes to making wise decisions. In life, we often face choices that require us to look beyond surface-level details. The Bible, with its precise and penetrating nature, helps us to make these decisions with clarity and wisdom. It guides us in understanding what is truly right and good, as opposed to what simply looks appealing or beneficial on the outside. Sometimes, what seems like the best choice according to the world's standards may not align with God's values. For instance, pursuing a certain career path might promise success and recognition, but, through God's Word, we may realize that it doesn't bring us closer to our true purpose. The Bible gives us the insight to distinguish between what is temporary and what has eternal significance, helping us to prioritize God's will above personal gain or comfort.

This surgical precision is a constant reminder that God cares about every detail of our lives. He is not distant or detached; He is intimately involved in who we are and who we are becoming. Just as a surgeon studies the patient and knows exactly where to operate, God knows us perfectly and knows exactly what needs to change in our lives for us to grow closer to Him. When we allow His Word to perform this kind of surgery in our hearts, we experience a deeper relationship with Him and a clearer sense of His presence and guidance. The process may be challenging, as it often requires us to confront uncomfortable truths and make difficult changes, but it is also profoundly rewarding. As we let go of hidden motives and align our desires with God's, we find a new sense of peace, purpose, and freedom. We begin to live with greater authenticity, knowing that our actions are driven by a genuine desire to serve and honor God rather than by personal ambition or fear.

In the end, the surgical precision of God's Word is a powerful tool for transformation. It doesn't just change what we do; it changes who we are. By cutting through layers of thought, revealing hidden motives, and addressing deep-seated issues, the Bible helps us become more like Christ. It purifies our hearts, sharpens our minds, and strengthens our faith, enabling us to live in a way that reflects God's love and truth to the world. This is the work of a lifetime, a continuous journey of letting God's Word shape us into the people He created us to be. And, as we open ourselves to this process, we find that each step brings us closer to the abundant life God promises—one that is filled with His peace, guided by His wisdom, and rooted in His unchanging love. The Word of God, with its unparalleled precision, is not only a guide but a means of true, lasting transformation that leads us to a life of purpose, integrity, and joy.

Chapter 4 – Strength

The strength of God's Word is an incredible, life-changing force that has the power to transform, renew, and build up people in ways they may never have imagined. When the Bible describes the Word as "powerful," it's not just a statement; it's a profound truth about the very nature of Scripture and the strength it holds to affect every area of our lives. Think about strength in the context of the things we see around us—how strong a tree's roots need to be to withstand storms, or the strength of a foundation that supports an entire building. God's Word has even greater strength; it is like a foundation that can support our lives through every challenge, storm, and difficulty. This strength doesn't come from human ideas or wisdom; it comes directly from God Himself. The words within the Bible are more than just text on a page; they are alive, filled with the power that comes from God, and when we read them, reflect on them, and apply them, they work within us to make us stronger, wiser, and more resilient. This is why so many people turn to the Bible not just for comfort but for strength, knowing that in its pages, they find the courage and wisdom to face life's hardest moments.

The strength of God's Word shows itself in many ways. For one, it has the power to change hearts and minds, giving people new perspectives, new hope, and a sense of purpose. There are countless stories of people who, feeling lost or broken, found their way back through the guidance of Scripture. It has the unique ability to speak directly to our hearts, providing exactly what we need, whether that's encouragement in times of despair or correction when we need to change our ways. The strength of the Bible also lies in its consistency; while life changes and the world around us shifts, God's Word remains the same, offering a stable, unchanging foundation for all who seek it. No matter what a person is going through, the Bible's truths apply—they offer insights, promises, and encouragement that can uplift and sustain anyone willing to listen and take them to heart. This is not just some temporary inspiration; it is a lasting, unbreakable source of strength that continues to work within us long after we've read it.

Another aspect of the Bible's strength is its power to reveal truth. Sometimes, we may be misled by our own thoughts, the opinions of others, or the confusing messages of the world, but God's Word cuts through all of that, providing clarity. It's like a bright light shining in a dark room, showing us the path forward and guiding us in the right direction. When we rely on Scripture, we can see our lives and choices more clearly, understanding what truly matters and what doesn't. This clarity gives us strength, too, because it removes uncertainty and helps us feel secure in the direction we're going. The Bible doesn't just tell us what's right; it gives us the strength to live it out, even when it's hard or goes against what others are doing. This kind of strength is particularly important in a world that often pulls us in different directions, where it's easy to feel pressured to go along with the crowd. But God's Word gives us the inner strength to stand firm, to make choices that honor Him, and to live with integrity and purpose.

God's Word also gives strength to face trials and suffering. Life is full of difficult times, and we all go through moments when we feel overwhelmed, sad, or even hopeless. In those times, Scripture offers hope and encouragement, reminding us of God's promises and love. Verses like "I can do all things through Christ who strengthens me" (Philippians 4:13) or "The Lord is my strength and my shield" (Psalm 28:7) are powerful reminders that we are never alone and that God is with us, providing the strength we need to endure. The Bible shows us that many others have gone through hard times—people like David, Job, and Paul—and they relied on God's strength to make it through. Reading their stories helps us realize that, no matter how tough our situation, God's strength is more than enough to carry us through. It encourages us to keep going, to trust that there is a purpose even in pain, and to know that God's power is made perfect in our weakness. This kind of strength isn't about having no struggles; it's about having the courage and resilience to keep moving forward, knowing that God is by our side.

Furthermore, the strength of God's Word builds us up spiritually, helping us to grow in faith and maturity. Just as physical exercise strengthens our bodies, reading and applying Scripture strengthens our spiritual lives. It teaches us to trust God more fully, to rely on Him in every situation, and to become more like Christ. Through the Bible, we learn patience, kindness, humility, and other qualities that make us stronger, not only in our faith but also in how we interact with others. When we are grounded in God's Word, we become better friends, family members, and community members because we are anchored in love and truth. This strength is not just for ourselves; it flows out to those around us, allowing us to support others and encourage them with the same strength we've found. In this way, the Bible doesn't just change individuals; it strengthens entire communities, bringing people together in love, faith, and mutual support.

The Bible's strength also lies in its ability to renew our minds. Sometimes, we carry negative thoughts, fears, or doubts that weigh us down and hold us back. God's Word has the power to transform the way we think, helping us to focus on truth and reject lies. Verses like "Be transformed by the renewing of your mind" (Romans 12:2) remind us that God wants to help us see things differently. When we fill our minds with Scripture, we begin to think in line with God's perspective, which gives us strength to overcome negative patterns and see ourselves and others through the lens of God's love. This renewal doesn't happen all at once; it's a daily process of choosing to meditate on God's promises and let them shape our outlook. As we do this, we find a new level of strength that helps us to stay positive, hopeful, and confident, even in tough situations.

Applying the strength of God's Word in our lives means turning to it regularly for guidance, encouragement, and support. It's like drinking water or eating food; we need it to sustain us. When we make reading the Bible a regular part of our routine, we build up our inner strength over time. The more we know Scripture, the more prepared we are to face life's challenges, because we have God's promises and wisdom stored up in our hearts. In moments of doubt, we can recall verses that remind us of God's faithfulness. In times of temptation, we can rely on verses that give us the strength to say no to things that would harm us. And in moments of fear, we can remember that God is our refuge and strength, a very present help in trouble (Psalm 46:1). This is why it's so important to stay connected to Scripture—it is a continuous source of strength that never runs dry.

In summary, the strength of God's Word is a powerful, unshakeable force that equips us to live with courage, wisdom, and faith. It changes us from the inside out, giving us a foundation that supports us through every high and low. It provides clarity and truth, helping us make wise choices, and gives us the courage to face trials and challenges with hope. It renews our minds, allowing us to see the world through God's perspective, and builds us up so that we can be a source of strength for others. By relying on Scripture as our source of strength, we tap into the incredible power of God's love, wisdom, and presence, experiencing a transformation that helps us to live fully and faithfully each day. This strength is available to everyone who seeks it, a gift from God that helps us become the people He created us to be. Through God's Word, we find the strength to overcome, to persevere, and to live with a sense of purpose and peace that only He can provide.

Chapter 5 - Searches Intentions

The idea that God's Word Searches Intentions is both amazing and humbling, showing how deeply the Bible can reach into our lives, even to the hidden places within our hearts and minds. When Scripture says that the Word is a "discerner of the thoughts and intents of the heart," it means that the Bible is not just a book of rules, stories, or teachings, but rather a powerful tool that examines and reveals what is truly within us. Unlike anything else, God's Word has a way of shining a light on our innermost thoughts, motivations, and desires, exposing the things we may not even be aware of or may try to hide. This unique ability of Scripture to "search intentions" means that when we read it with an open heart, it helps us see ourselves more clearly and honestly. Sometimes, we may believe we're doing something for the right reasons, but God's Word can reveal if we have hidden motives that are more about serving ourselves than others or God. For instance, we might think we're being generous or helpful, but deep down, perhaps we're looking for praise or recognition. The Bible has a way of exposing these motives, not to shame us, but to help us grow, correct, and align ourselves more closely with God's will. In this way, the Word acts almost like a mirror, showing us who we truly are inside and helping us become more aware of areas we may need to change or improve.

The ability of God's Word to search our intentions is powerful because our intentions shape our actions and define our character. When we let the Bible examine our intentions, it helps us understand why we do what we do. Are we acting out of love, kindness, and faith, or are there selfish desires hidden beneath the surface? The Bible teaches that God cares not only about our actions but also about the motives behind them, which is why examining our intentions is so important. For example, giving to others is a good action, but if our intention is to gain something in return or to look good in front of others, then the action loses its true value in God's eyes. God desires us to act from a place of genuine love and humility, and His Word helps us recognize when we might be falling short of that ideal. As we read and reflect on Scripture, it can bring up feelings, thoughts, or memories that show us where we may need to adjust our attitude or motives. This process can be challenging because it asks us to look honestly at ourselves, but it is also incredibly rewarding as it leads us to become better people, more aligned with God's character and purposes.

One of the beautiful aspects of letting God's Word search our intentions is that it's a gentle but firm process. God doesn't expose our hidden motives to make us feel bad; He does it to help us grow in love, faith, and humility. This search for intentions is like having a wise friend who lovingly points out areas we might overlook or misunderstand. It's not about punishment; it's about guidance and growth. For instance, we may think we're being honest, but God's Word may show us areas where we're still holding back or not being completely truthful. Or, we may believe we're being patient, only for Scripture to reveal impatience hidden in our hearts. This process teaches us humility, as we realize that we're always in need of God's wisdom and correction. By allowing Scripture to uncover these hidden areas, we become more authentic and sincere in our faith, living out the values we truly believe in rather than simply going through the motions. This kind of growth is what God desires for us, and the Word is a tool that He uses to make this growth possible, refining us like gold in a fire.

Another aspect of the Bible's ability to search our intentions is that it prepares us to serve others more genuinely. When our intentions are pure and rooted in God's love, our actions naturally reflect that love to those around us. In relationships, whether with family, friends, or strangers, having genuine intentions allows us to build trust and connect with people on a deeper level. The Bible's guidance helps us approach others with true compassion rather than self-interest. For example, instead of helping someone just to feel good about ourselves, Scripture reminds us to help because it's the right thing to do, reflecting Christ's love. This change in mindset makes a big difference in how we interact with others. People can often sense when someone's kindness is genuine, and it creates an environment where God's love and grace can flourish. The Bible's role in shaping our intentions is essential in creating these positive relationships, helping us serve others without seeking anything in return.

The Word's ability to discern thoughts and intentions also provides a strong foundation for making wise decisions. Life is filled with choices, and sometimes it's difficult to know what the best path is. But when we let the Bible guide us, it helps clarify our motives and keeps us focused on what's truly important. For example, when making a decision about a career, relationship, or personal goal, Scripture can help us examine why we want what we want. Are we choosing a job because it aligns with our gifts and serves God's purpose, or is it because we're seeking prestige or material wealth? Are we pursuing a relationship out of love and commitment, or are we afraid of loneliness or looking for validation? The Bible's wisdom can help us untangle these complex feelings, guiding us toward choices that honor God and reflect His character. This doesn't mean every decision will be easy, but it does mean we'll have a clearer sense of direction and purpose, rooted in God's truth rather than fleeting desires.

The process of examining our intentions through God's Word also brings us closer to God Himself. As we become more honest with ourselves and align our motives with God's will, we draw nearer to His heart. God desires a close relationship with us, and that relationship grows deeper when we're open and honest about our intentions. Reading and reflecting on Scripture becomes a time of self-discovery and transformation, where we not only learn more about God but also learn more about ourselves. This honesty before God allows us to experience His grace and forgiveness in a profound way. When we acknowledge our hidden motives and ask God to help us change, we receive His guidance and strength to make those changes. It's a humbling but beautiful experience to realize that, even with our imperfections, God loves us deeply and wants to help us grow. Each time we open the Bible with a willing heart, we invite God to shape us and to bring us closer to the person He created us to be.

Furthermore, using the Bible to search our intentions teaches us the value of integrity and authenticity. In a world where appearances often matter more than reality, it's easy to fall into the trap of doing things just for show. But God's Word reminds us that what's in our hearts matters most to Him. By examining our intentions, we learn to live with integrity, making choices that reflect our true values rather than what might look good to others. This kind of authenticity is freeing because it removes the need to constantly seek approval or recognition. We become more focused on pleasing God, who sees and understands our hearts better than anyone else. This shift in perspective gives us confidence and peace, knowing that we're living for something greater than ourselves. We don't have to hide behind a mask or pretend to be something we're not; instead, we can be open and honest, trusting that God's love for us is unconditional.

Finally, allowing Scripture to search our intentions prepares us to face life's challenges with a stronger, clearer sense of purpose. When we understand our true motives and align them with God's will, we are better equipped to handle difficult situations. Challenges will come, but with a foundation built on genuine intentions and God's guidance, we're able to stay focused on what truly matters. This inner clarity helps us resist distractions and avoid actions driven by fear, pride, or selfishness. Instead, we face challenges with courage and humility, knowing that our motives are pure and our actions are grounded in God's truth. This strength allows us to persevere through hardships without losing sight of who we are or what we stand for. In moments of temptation or pressure, the Bible's guidance helps us stay true to ourselves and to God, ensuring that our intentions remain aligned with His purposes.

In summary, the Bible's ability to search our intentions is a powerful gift that helps us grow closer to God, understand ourselves better, and live with integrity and purpose. It shines a light on our hidden motives, guiding us to act with sincerity and love. By regularly reflecting on Scripture and allowing it to examine our hearts, we become more authentic, more compassionate, and more aligned with God's will. This process is challenging but rewarding, leading us to a life that is more grounded, meaningful, and connected to God's love.

Chapter 6 - Spiritual Depth

The concept of Spiritual Depth is one of the most profound and meaningful aspects of God's Word. When we say that the Bible addresses the "thoughts and intents" of the heart, we are talking about how it reaches down into the deepest parts of who we are, impacting not just our actions or words, but the very core of our being – our beliefs, values, desires, and motivations. Unlike any other book, the Bible speaks to what lies beneath the surface. It doesn't just give us rules to follow or stories to read; it digs deep into our souls, touching the parts of us that we might not even fully understand ourselves. Scripture has the unique ability to reveal to us our true selves, exposing our fears, our insecurities, our pride, and even our deepest longings. It helps us to see ourselves the way God sees us, bringing to light both the beauty and the brokenness within. This depth is powerful because it allows for real transformation. Instead of just changing outward behaviors, God's Word reaches into our innermost beliefs and values, guiding us to align them with His truth. This means that the Bible isn't just about learning facts or rules; it's about developing a relationship with God that transforms us from the inside out, impacting everything about how we live, think, and love.

One of the remarkable things about the Bible's spiritual depth is how it adapts to speak to each person uniquely, no matter where they are in life. Whether someone is new to faith or has been following God for years, Scripture has a way of reaching them at their level, revealing something new each time it is read. For some, it might bring comfort and peace, while for others, it might challenge and convict, calling them to a higher standard. This depth is why people can read the same passage multiple times throughout their lives and continually find new insights, answers, and encouragement. It speaks to our situations, helping us understand our experiences through God's perspective and teaching us lessons that we need in each season of life. When we face sorrow, the Bible speaks of God's comfort; when we're confused, it provides wisdom; and when we're joyful, it reminds us to give thanks. This ability to adapt and speak personally to each reader demonstrates that the Bible isn't just words on a page; it's a living document, active and relevant, powered by God's Spirit to reach us in the deepest ways possible.

The Bible's spiritual depth also means that it touches on all aspects of our identity, not just the spiritual parts. It reaches into our minds, our emotions, our relationships, and our sense of purpose, bringing everything into alignment with God's truth. This is important because, as humans, we often separate our lives into compartments—work, family, faith, friends—but God's Word shows us that everything is connected. When we let the Bible influence our core beliefs, it affects every other area of life. For example, when we understand from Scripture that we are loved unconditionally by God, it changes the way we see ourselves and how we interact with others. We become more compassionate, more forgiving, and more secure in who we are. This deep transformation means that the Bible isn't just something we read on Sundays or when we're in trouble; it becomes the foundation of our entire life, guiding our decisions, shaping our character, and giving us a clear sense of who we are and why we are here.

Allowing Scripture to guide our innermost beliefs and values requires us to be open and vulnerable, letting God's Word examine parts of us that we might otherwise ignore or protect. This is not always an easy process. Often, the Bible challenges our assumptions, confronts our biases, and invites us to let go of things that we hold dear but that might not align with God's will. For instance, we might believe that success is measured by wealth or popularity, but Scripture teaches us to value humility, generosity, and service. Similarly, we might have a habit of holding grudges or seeking revenge, but the Bible calls us to forgive and seek peace. These teachings can be difficult to accept, especially when they go against what society values, but this is where the spiritual depth of the Bible truly shines. It doesn't just tell us what we want to hear; it tells us what we need to hear in order to grow closer to God and to become more like Christ. This process of realignment, though challenging, is deeply rewarding, as it brings us into harmony with God's design for our lives and fills us with a sense of purpose and peace that nothing else can provide.

The depth of Scripture also speaks to the idea of spiritual maturity. Just as people grow physically and emotionally, we also grow spiritually, and the Bible is essential to this growth. When we first come to faith, we might understand the basics of God's love and forgiveness, but as we dive deeper into Scripture, we begin to see the complexities of God's character and the richness of His plans for humanity. We start to grasp the depth of His grace, the strength of His justice, and the boundlessness of His mercy. This spiritual maturity doesn't happen overnight; it's a lifelong journey of studying, reflecting, and applying God's Word to our lives. The more we read and reflect on Scripture, the more we understand about who God is and who He calls us to be. This growth isn't just for our benefit; it equips us to help others, to serve our communities, and to be a light in the world. As we mature in our faith, guided by the depth of Scripture, we become stronger, wiser, and more resilient, able to face life's challenges with confidence and hope.

The depth of God's Word is also a source of great comfort and encouragement, especially in times of hardship. When we go through difficult seasons, the Bible speaks directly to our pain, offering words of hope and reassurance. It reminds us that God is close to the brokenhearted, that He will never leave us nor forsake us, and that He works all things for the good of those who love Him. These truths reach deep into our hearts, giving us strength and peace even when our circumstances are tough. The Bible doesn't promise a life free of pain, but it promises that we are never alone and that God's love and grace are sufficient for every trial. This comfort is not shallow or fleeting; it's rooted in the eternal promises of God, providing a solid foundation that we can cling to no matter what we face. Knowing that God understands our struggles and is with us every step of the way brings a sense of calm and assurance that nothing else can provide.

Another aspect of the Bible's spiritual depth is its ability to answer life's big questions. People have always wrestled with questions like "Why am I here?" "What is the purpose of life?" and "What happens after we die?" While the world offers many theories and philosophies, the Bible provides clear, profound answers that satisfy the soul's deepest longings. It teaches us that we are created in God's image, that we are loved by Him, and that our purpose is to know Him, love Him, and reflect His love to others. It assures us that there is life beyond this world, a life where we will be united with God and free from all pain and suffering. These answers give us a sense of direction and meaning, helping us to live with purpose and hope. The Bible's teachings on these big questions are not just abstract ideas; they are truths that shape the way we live, giving us a reason to get up each day and to approach life with joy and gratitude.

Ultimately, the depth of God's Word is about relationship—our relationship with God and with others. As we let Scripture influence our innermost beliefs, we draw closer to God, understanding more of His heart and His desires for us. This relationship is not about following rules or checking off religious tasks; it's about knowing and loving God, and letting His love transform us. Through the Bible, we come to see God not as a distant figure but as a loving Father who cares deeply about every aspect of our lives. This depth of relationship is what gives us strength, courage, and hope, no matter what we face. And as we grow closer to God, we also become better at loving others. The Bible teaches us to be patient, kind, forgiving, and generous, qualities that deepen our relationships and help us to build stronger, healthier communities. The depth of Scripture leads us to live lives that reflect God's love and grace, impacting not only our own lives but also the lives of those around us.

In conclusion, the spiritual depth of God's Word is a treasure that reaches into every part of who we are. It addresses the thoughts and intents of our hearts, guiding us to align our beliefs and values with God's truth. This depth brings transformation, maturity, comfort, and purpose, helping us to live lives that honor God and bring joy to those around us. By allowing Scripture to shape our innermost selves, we find a depth of peace, love, and fulfillment that nothing else in the world can offer.

Chapter 7 - Source of Life

The Bible as a Source of Life is a concept that shows just how powerful and essential God's Word is for us. When Scripture says that the Word is "quick," it doesn't mean fast; it means alive. The Bible is not just a book full of old stories, rules, or wisdom from the past. It is a living force, filled with God's Spirit, that brings life to anyone who reads it, listens to it, and believes in it. This is why people often call it the "living Word of God." It is alive in a way that other books aren't. Its words continue to speak to people across different times, places, and cultures. It has the power to comfort, guide, correct, and inspire, not just once but over and over again. Because it is alive, it connects directly to our hearts and spirits, speaking to us in ways that are fresh and personal. Each time we read it, God's Word can meet us exactly where we are, whether we are happy, sad, confused, or in need of direction. This life-giving quality of the Bible makes it unlike any other book because it can transform lives, bring hope to those who feel lost, and renew people's strength in times of difficulty. Just as we need food and water to keep our bodies alive, we need the Bible to keep our spiritual lives healthy and growing. The Bible is like spiritual food, nourishing our souls and giving us the energy we need to face life's challenges and to live with purpose.

God's Word gives life by renewing our minds, helping us see the world and ourselves in new ways. Sometimes, our thoughts get filled with negative or harmful ideas that make us feel anxious, sad, or unworthy. But when we turn to the Bible, it brings us back to the truth of who God is and who we are. It reminds us that we are loved by God, that we have a purpose, and that we are never alone. It helps us focus on what is good and true, lifting us up when we feel down and filling us with peace when we feel worried. This is one of the reasons why so many people find comfort in the Psalms or strength in the words of Jesus. The Bible's words are like a refreshing drink of water for our minds, helping us to let go of the things that drag us down and filling us with hope and courage instead. Each verse and story in the Bible has the power to remind us of God's promises, which are always reliable. It's not just about making us feel better; it's about giving us a foundation that we can rely on, a solid ground that helps us stay strong and steady even when life gets hard.

The Bible is a source of life because it connects us directly to God, who is the ultimate source of all life. Through reading and meditating on Scripture, we open ourselves up to God's presence and His Spirit. It's like opening a window to let in fresh air. When we spend time in the Word, it fills us with God's Spirit, which renews our hearts and minds, helping us to grow closer to Him and to understand His love and His plans for us. This connection to God through His Word brings joy, peace, and strength that the world can't offer. Just as plants need sunlight to grow and thrive, our souls need the light of God's Word to flourish. Without it, we may feel empty or disconnected, but with it, we feel alive, refreshed, and full of purpose. The Bible doesn't just give us knowledge; it helps us experience God's presence in a real and personal way, guiding us through life's ups and downs. This living connection is why so many people turn to the Bible not only in times of crisis but also in their daily lives, knowing that it has the power to sustain them and give them the life they need.

Another way the Bible serves as a source of life is by giving us wisdom and direction for our everyday decisions. Life can be confusing, and we often face choices that are difficult to make. But the Bible is filled with God's wisdom, which helps us see things more clearly and make choices that lead to a better, more fulfilling life. It teaches us how to treat others, how to handle money, how to deal with anger or fear, and how to live in a way that honors God. This guidance isn't just for big decisions; it's for the small, daily choices that shape who we are and how we live. By following the Bible's teachings, we find a path that leads to true joy and peace, avoiding the traps and mistakes that often cause pain or regret. The Bible's wisdom is timeless; even though it was written long ago, its principles still apply to our modern lives because they are rooted in God's unchanging truth. When we live by these principles, we experience a kind of freedom and satisfaction that can only come from living the way we were meant to live.

The Bible also gives life by encouraging us to grow and improve. It doesn't just tell us what we want to hear; it challenges us to be better. When we read verses that speak about kindness, forgiveness, patience, or humility, they inspire us to become more like Christ. This process of growth can be hard, as it often means letting go of selfish desires or bad habits, but it is deeply rewarding. By following the Bible's guidance, we become stronger, more compassionate, and more joyful people. The changes that God's Word brings are not just surface-level; they go deep, affecting our hearts and shaping our character. This is why people who spend time in the Bible often find that they become more patient, more loving, and more at peace over time. It's not just that they are following rules; it's that God's Word is transforming them from the inside out, making them into the people God created them to be. This transformation is a source of life because it fills us with a sense of purpose and joy that goes beyond temporary happiness.

The Bible as a source of life is also evident in the way it brings people together. When people study God's Word together, it creates a sense of community and belonging. Sharing Scripture, discussing its meaning, and encouraging each other through it helps build strong relationships that are based on love and truth. This sense of community is life-giving because it reminds us that we are not alone. We are part of a larger family of believers who support each other, pray for each other, and help each other grow. This community, rooted in God's Word, becomes a place where people can find acceptance, love, and support, especially during difficult times. It's a place where people can be honest about their struggles and find encouragement to keep going. The life that the Bible brings is not just for individuals; it's for communities and families, helping them to grow together in love and unity.

The Bible's power to give life is also seen in its ability to provide hope. Life is often filled with challenges, pain, and uncertainty, and it can be easy to feel discouraged. But the Bible is filled with promises of hope, reminding us that God is with us, that He loves us, and that He has a plan for us. Verses like "For I know the plans I have for you, says the Lord, plans for welfare and not for evil, to give you a future and a hope" (Jeremiah 29:11) are a reminder that our lives have purpose and meaning. This hope is life-giving because it gives us the strength to keep going, even when things are tough. It reminds us that there is more to life than our current struggles and that God is working in all things for our good. This hope, rooted in God's promises, gives us a firm foundation to stand on, helping us to face each day with confidence and peace.

In conclusion, the Bible as a Source of Life is one of the most powerful aspects of our faith. It is not just a book to be read; it is a living Word that brings life, hope, strength, and purpose to all who embrace it. By letting the Bible into our hearts and minds, we experience a deep and lasting connection to God, which fills us with peace, joy, and strength that nothing else can provide. It is our guide, our comfort, our encouragement, and our source of wisdom. The Bible is truly alive, and it continues to speak to us, renew us, and give us life each day.

Chapter 8 - Self-Examination

The concept of Self-Examination through Scripture is a powerful tool for personal growth and understanding our true character. The Bible is unique in that it doesn't just tell us what we want to hear or give us surface-level guidance. Instead, it goes much deeper, examining the thoughts and intentions of our hearts, helping us to understand who we really are beneath our actions, words, and appearances. When we use Scripture for self-examination, it's like holding up a mirror that reflects not only what we show to the world but also what lies hidden inside. The Bible discerns, or understands, the true intentions behind our thoughts and actions, which allows us to gain a clearer, more honest view of ourselves. This process of looking inward isn't about finding flaws to dwell on or feeling guilty, but rather about growth, honesty, and becoming more aligned with God's will. It reveals both our strengths and our weaknesses, areas of our lives that may need change, and aspects that we might overlook in the busyness of daily life. This self-examination is essential because it helps us understand what drives us, what we value most, and where we may be falling short of the life God desires for us. By using Scripture as a guide for self-reflection, we open ourselves up to real transformation, a process that brings us closer to God and helps us live more meaningful, authentic lives.

One of the most important things about self-examination through Scripture is that it provides a standard of truth that doesn't change. In a world where values and opinions are constantly shifting, it can be difficult to know what is right or true. However, the Bible gives us a constant, unchanging foundation, rooted in God's truth, that we can rely on to guide our lives. When we use this foundation to examine ourselves, we're not basing our understanding of who we are on society's standards, popular trends, or even our own feelings, which can often be unreliable. Instead, we're using God's Word as a solid and trustworthy standard, which helps us see ourselves through His eyes. This allows us to approach self-examination with a sense of stability and confidence, knowing that we're being measured against the eternal values of love, kindness, humility, patience, and faith. This truth can be both comforting and challenging. It comforts us by reassuring us of God's love and forgiveness, but it also challenges us by pointing out areas where we need to grow or change. Through this lens of Scripture, we learn that true self-examination isn't about comparing ourselves to others or achieving perfection; it's about growing closer to God and becoming the people He created us to be.

Scripture for self-examination helps us look beyond the surface and uncover hidden motivations and desires that may be influencing our actions. For example, we may think we're being generous when we give to others, but the Bible might help us recognize that our giving is sometimes driven by a desire for praise or recognition rather than pure kindness. Or we might believe we're acting out of love, but upon deeper reflection through Scripture, we might see traces of selfishness or pride in our actions. The Bible helps us to uncover these hidden aspects of ourselves in a way that no other tool can, allowing us to deal with them honestly and seek God's help to change. This process of uncovering hidden motives can be uncomfortable because it requires humility and a willingness to admit that we're not perfect. However, it is also incredibly freeing, because when we acknowledge these things, we can begin to work on them with God's guidance and support. By allowing Scripture to highlight these deeper parts of our character, we are better able to align our actions with our faith, making sure that what we do truly reflects God's love and truth.

Self-examination through Scripture also helps us grow in areas that we might not even realize need attention. Life is often busy, and we can get so caught up in routines and responsibilities that we don't stop to think about whether we're truly living according to God's will. Reading the Bible encourages us to pause, reflect, and consider whether our choices, habits, and relationships are aligned with the values of love, integrity, and compassion that God calls us to uphold. For example, we might read a verse about forgiveness and realize that we're holding onto bitterness toward someone, or we might come across a passage about humility and see that we've been acting out of pride without even realizing it. These moments of insight are opportunities for growth, as they help us identify areas of our lives that we can bring into closer alignment with God's Word. By regularly using Scripture for self-examination, we stay connected to God's guidance, allowing Him to shape our hearts and lives in ways that help us grow stronger, kinder, and more faithful.

Self-examination through Scripture also builds humility, teaching us that we all have room to grow and that no one is perfect. The Bible reminds us that we all fall short in some way, but it also reassures us of God's grace and mercy. This combination of truth and grace allows us to look at our flaws and weaknesses without fear or shame, knowing that God's love for us is unchanging. It encourages us to be humble, to admit our mistakes, and to seek forgiveness when we need it. In a world that often pressures us to appear strong and flawless, the Bible gives us permission to be real, to acknowledge our struggles, and to rely on God's strength rather than our own. This humility is essential for personal growth because it opens the door for God to work in our lives, transforming us in ways we could never achieve on our own. By embracing self-examination with a humble heart, we become more receptive to God's guidance, allowing Him to lead us toward greater maturity, wisdom, and love.

One of the most powerful aspects of self-examination through Scripture is that it not only helps us identify areas for personal growth but also strengthens our relationship with God. As we read the Bible and reflect on its teachings, we gain a deeper understanding of God's character, His love for us, and His desires for our lives. This knowledge helps us to trust Him more fully, knowing that His guidance is for our good and His correction is a sign of His care. Self-examination isn't just about improving ourselves; it's about drawing closer to God, building a relationship that is honest, open, and deeply rooted in faith. When we allow God's Word to shape our hearts, we begin to experience His presence in new and meaningful ways, finding comfort, strength, and encouragement that help us through every season of life. This closeness to God is one of the greatest gifts of self-examination, as it fills us with a sense of peace and purpose that only comes from knowing and following Him.

Finally, self-examination through Scripture helps us to be better friends, family members, and members of our communities. As we grow in self-awareness and become more aligned with God's love, we are better able to serve others, to show compassion, and to build relationships that reflect God's grace. By examining our hearts, we learn to let go of selfishness, jealousy, and anger, replacing them with kindness, forgiveness, and understanding. This transformation doesn't just impact our own lives; it has a ripple effect, spreading God's love to everyone we meet. When we allow Scripture to guide our thoughts and actions, we become a light to others, a source of encouragement and hope that points people toward God's love. This is the ultimate goal of self-examination through God's Word: to become a person who not only grows closer to God but also brings His love and truth into the world in real, tangible ways.

Chapter 9 - Separates Sin

The power of God's Word to Separate Sin from our lives is one of its most transformative and freeing qualities. The Bible is described as "piercing" and "dividing," which means it doesn't just skim the surface of our thoughts and actions; it goes deep into the very core of who we are, cutting through all our defenses, distractions, and denials to reveal what truly lies within. Unlike anything else, God's Word is like a spiritual sword, sharp and precise, able to expose even the hidden sins we may not want to face or may not even realize are there. When we read Scripture with an open heart, it acts as a mirror that shows us our true selves, including the parts that need changing. It exposes sin for what it is, removing any excuses or justifications we might make and allowing us to see our wrongdoings clearly. This process is sometimes uncomfortable because it requires us to confront things we may have tried to hide or ignore, but it is also incredibly necessary and life-changing. By shining a light on these areas, God's Word helps us recognize the thoughts, actions, and attitudes that separate us from Him, making us aware of how sin impacts our relationship with Him, with others, and even with ourselves.

God's Word doesn't just stop at pointing out sin; it empowers us to do something about it. It convicts us in a way that is gentle yet firm, allowing us to feel the weight of our wrongdoings without crushing us under guilt. Instead, it invites us to seek forgiveness and make changes, leading us on a path to freedom from the chains of sin. The Bible's clarity on sin is like a guide, showing us the behaviors and choices that harm us and lead us away from God's love and purpose for our lives. For example, we may read verses about honesty and realize that we've been hiding truths or exaggerating to make ourselves look better. Or we might come across teachings on kindness and realize that our words have been harsh or judgmental. This clarity brings about conviction, a gentle but persistent reminder from God that we need to turn away from these actions and align ourselves more closely with His values. This conviction is not about feeling ashamed; it's about feeling motivated to grow, to improve, and to become more like the person God created us to be. Scripture doesn't leave us in our sin; it calls us to rise above it, to seek God's help in overcoming it, and to find strength in His forgiveness and grace.

The Bible's ability to separate us from sin also means it provides a path to cleansing and renewal. As we read God's Word and allow it to work in us, it purifies our hearts and minds, helping us let go of sinful habits and thoughts that have held us back. Just as water cleanses dirt from our bodies, the words of Scripture cleanse us spiritually, washing away the guilt and grime that sin leaves behind. This cleansing isn't a one-time event; it's an ongoing process, as each time we read the Bible, it continues to reveal new areas in which we can grow. It's like peeling back layers, uncovering deeper issues and hidden attitudes that we might not have been ready to address before. This process of cleansing and renewal transforms us over time, helping us to think and act in ways that reflect God's goodness. As we continue to study Scripture, we become more sensitive to the presence of sin in our lives and more willing to remove it. Our hearts become aligned with God's will, making it easier to say no to temptation and to choose actions that honor Him. This transformation isn't something we achieve by our own strength; it's the work of God's Word within us, steadily and powerfully changing us from the inside out.

One of the reasons God's Word is so effective in separating us from sin is because it gives us a clear standard of right and wrong. In a world where morals and values are often blurred or subjective, the Bible provides an unchanging truth that we can rely on. It shows us clearly what pleases God and what doesn't, removing any confusion about what is truly right or wrong. When we read about God's commandments, we see that His guidelines are not there to restrict us but to protect us, guiding us toward a life of purpose, peace, and joy. This standard helps us understand why certain actions, thoughts, or habits are harmful and why we need to let them go. For instance, the Bible teaches that holding onto anger or bitterness harms our hearts, while forgiveness brings freedom. Understanding this truth helps us see the importance of letting go of grudges, not because it's easy, but because it brings us closer to God's peace. God's Word doesn't just tell us to avoid sin; it explains why sin is harmful and shows us a better way to live. This guidance is like a light in the darkness, helping us navigate the challenges and temptations of life with confidence and clarity.

Seeking Scripture to convict and cleanse areas of sin in our lives is an essential part of growing in faith and building a closer relationship with God. When we approach the Bible with humility and a willingness to be changed, we invite God to do a deep work within us. This openness allows us to see our sins not as isolated mistakes but as obstacles that keep us from fully experiencing God's love and grace. By allowing Scripture to reveal these areas, we are empowered to address them head-on, seeking God's help to overcome and remove anything that separates us from Him. The Bible gives us practical tools for dealing with sin, such as prayer, repentance, and accountability, helping us to break free from patterns that have held us captive. Through regular reading and reflection, we learn to recognize temptation more quickly and to rely on God's strength rather than our own. Each time we confront a sin and choose to turn away from it, we become stronger, more resilient, and more attuned to God's voice. This process of separating from sin doesn't just change our actions; it transforms our hearts, making us more compassionate, patient, and loving individuals who reflect God's character in everything we do.

One of the most beautiful aspects of God's Word separating us from sin is that it leads us to experience God's grace and forgiveness in a profound way. When we see our sins clearly and understand the weight of our wrongdoings, we also come to appreciate the depth of God's mercy. The Bible assures us that no matter how far we have strayed, God's love is always there, ready to welcome us back and to forgive us completely. This forgiveness is not something we earn; it's a gift that God offers freely to all who repent and seek Him. Experiencing this grace transforms us, filling us with gratitude and a desire to live in a way that honors God. We begin to understand that separating from sin is not just about avoiding punishment; it's about stepping into a life filled with God's presence, peace, and purpose. This journey of separating from sin brings us closer to God, helping us to see Him not as a distant judge but as a loving Father who wants the best for us.

In conclusion, the Bible's ability to separate us from sin is a powerful and essential aspect of our spiritual growth. It exposes sin clearly, convicts us to change, cleanses us from guilt, and guides us toward a life that is free from the bondage of sin. By regularly seeking Scripture, we allow God's Word to work within us, transforming us into people who reflect His love, truth, and goodness in all that we do. This journey of separating from sin is not always easy, but it is deeply rewarding, bringing us closer to God and helping us to live lives of purpose, joy, and freedom.

Chapter 10 – Sanctification

The concept of Sanctification through God's Word is a powerful journey of spiritual growth and transformation, one that helps believers become more like Christ by setting them apart for holy purposes. Sanctification is all about purification and refinement, and it is something that takes time, commitment, and the willingness to let God's Word do its work within us. The Bible describes itself as sharper than a two-edged sword, meaning it can pierce deeply into our hearts, minds, and souls, cutting away anything that doesn't align with God's will. Just like a blade used to refine and shape a material, God's Word has a purifying effect on us, chipping away at our imperfections, sinful tendencies, and flawed thoughts. This sharpness of Scripture allows it to reach into every hidden corner of our hearts, revealing areas we may need to change, habits we need to break, and attitudes we need to adjust. The Word doesn't just tell us how to act; it transforms us from the inside out, helping us become more aligned with God's heart and purposes. When we open ourselves up to the sanctifying power of Scripture, we allow God to shape us into people who reflect His love, kindness, patience, and holiness in every aspect of our lives. This process may be challenging, as it often requires us to let go of things we've held onto or change parts of ourselves that we're comfortable with, but it is essential for anyone who truly desires to follow Christ.

God's Word sanctifies us by setting us apart from the world, giving us a different set of values and priorities that are rooted in His truth. While the world might prioritize success, wealth, and pleasure, the Bible teaches us to value love, humility, service, and faith. This difference in values is what makes believers distinct, and it is part of the sanctification process. When we let Scripture guide our thoughts and actions, we become more aware of the things in our lives that might pull us away from God's purposes. For example, if we are tempted to seek approval from others or pursue things for selfish gain, the

Bible reminds us to focus on serving God and others rather than ourselves. This guidance helps us resist the temptations and distractions of the world, strengthening our commitment to live lives that honor God. Sanctification is about becoming "set apart" not because we are better than anyone else, but because we are called to live according to a higher standard that reflects God's character. This calling is a privilege, but it also comes with responsibility, as we seek to live in a way that shows others the difference that Christ makes in our lives.

The sanctifying power of God's Word also brings about a deep and lasting change in our character. As we spend time reading, studying, and reflecting on Scripture, we begin to see a transformation in our thoughts, words, and actions. We start to respond to situations with more patience, to speak with more kindness, and to approach challenges with faith rather than fear. This change doesn't happen overnight; it's a gradual process that requires consistent effort and a willingness to let God's Word work in us. The Bible serves as a mirror, showing us where we fall short and where we need to grow, but it also gives us the tools and encouragement to make those changes. It teaches us how to forgive when we've been wronged, to love even those who are difficult to love, and to trust in God's plan even when we don't understand it. Each time we apply Scripture to our lives, we take another step toward becoming more like Christ. This is the essence of sanctification—allowing God to mold us into the people He created us to be, so that our lives can reflect His goodness and grace to the world around us.

One of the most beautiful aspects of sanctification is that it brings us closer to God. As we let Scripture purify our hearts and minds, we become more sensitive to His presence and more aware of His guidance in our lives. The things that once distracted us or pulled us away from God start to lose their appeal, and our desire to know and follow Him grows stronger. This closeness to God is one of the greatest rewards of sanctification, as it fills us with peace, joy, and purpose that nothing else can provide. The more we are sanctified, the more we understand God's love for us and His plan for our lives, which helps us to trust Him more fully and to surrender our own plans and desires to Him. Sanctification helps us to see God not just as a distant authority figure, but as a loving Father who cares deeply about every detail of our lives. This relationship is at the heart of what it means to be set apart for holy purposes, as we learn to rely on God's strength and wisdom rather than our own.

Allowing Scripture to guide us in becoming more Christ-like also impacts our relationships with others. As we grow in sanctification, we learn to treat people with the same love, respect, and compassion that Christ showed. This change in how we interact with others is one of the most visible signs of sanctification, as it reflects the heart of Jesus in a world that often lacks kindness and empathy. The Bible teaches us to love our neighbors as ourselves, to forgive those who hurt us, and to serve others with humility. These are not easy things to do, especially when we feel wronged or misunderstood, but they are part of the sanctifying work that God is doing in us. When we allow Scripture to shape our hearts, we become more willing to put aside our pride and ego, choosing instead to show grace and understanding. This doesn't mean that we become passive or allow others to take advantage of us; it means that we choose to respond with love and patience, even in difficult situations, because we know that this is what Christ would do. Through sanctification, we become peacemakers, encouragers, and sources of hope for those around us, showing the world what it means to live a life that is dedicated to God.

The process of sanctification is also deeply personal, as it addresses each individual's unique struggles, weaknesses, and strengths. God knows each of us intimately, and He uses His Word to speak to us in ways that are specific to our own lives. For one person, sanctification might mean learning to let go of anger and embrace forgiveness. For another, it might involve developing patience or learning to trust God's timing. The Bible meets us wherever we are, providing wisdom, correction, and encouragement that helps us grow in the areas where we need it most. This personal nature of sanctification is what makes it so powerful, as it shows that God is not interested in a one-size-fits-all approach; He cares about each of us individually and works in our hearts according to our unique journeys. As we go through this process, we come to see that sanctification is not about perfection; it's about progress. It's about becoming more like Christ, one step at a time, and trusting that God is with us every step of the way.

In conclusion, the sanctifying power of God's Word is a gift that purifies, transforms, and sets us apart for holy purposes. It's a lifelong journey that draws us closer to God, strengthens our character, and helps us reflect Christ in our daily lives. By allowing Scripture to guide us in this process, we become people who are not only changed internally but who also make a positive impact on the world around us. This is the true beauty of sanctification—a transformation that brings us into deeper relationship with God and enables us to live lives that are dedicated to His glory.

Chapter 11 – Sustenance

The concept of Sustenance in terms of God's Word is incredibly powerful and essential for a strong and healthy spiritual life. Just as our bodies need physical food to survive, grow, and stay energized, our souls need spiritual food to remain strong, resilient, and connected to God. The Bible is described as the ultimate source of spiritual nourishment, meaning it provides the support, wisdom, and guidance our spirits need each day. Without it, we can feel weak, lost, and even disconnected from our faith. When we talk about sustenance from God's Word, we're not just saying that the Bible has good advice or interesting stories; we're saying that it is the foundation that feeds our soul, giving us what we need to face challenges, make wise decisions, and grow closer to God. Reading the Bible daily is like a meal for our spirit—it refreshes us, strengthens us, and keeps us spiritually healthy. When we skip spending time in Scripture, it's like skipping meals for our soul. Just as we wouldn't expect our physical bodies to feel strong and energized if we skipped eating, we can't expect our spiritual lives to flourish if we aren't feeding on God's Word regularly. This spiritual nourishment is what keeps us rooted in God's truth, especially when life gets difficult or confusing.

One of the amazing things about the Bible as a source of sustenance is that it meets us exactly where we are. No matter what we're going through—whether we're happy, struggling, tired, or excited—Scripture has something to offer. When we're joyful, it helps us celebrate and give thanks to God. When we're sad or going through a hard time, it comforts us and reminds us that we are never alone. When we need guidance, it provides wisdom, showing us the right path to take. This adaptability makes Scripture a reliable source of strength and hope, no matter the situation. For example, the Psalms offer words of encouragement and peace for those who are feeling anxious, while the teachings of Jesus provide direction and purpose for those looking for meaning. This personalized nourishment is what makes the Bible so special; it's not just words on a page—it's a living, active source of encouragement and support that speaks to each of us individually. This sustenance from Scripture is what keeps our spirits thriving and growing, ensuring that we are spiritually fed and ready to face whatever life throws our way.

God's Word as sustenance also plays a crucial role in building our spiritual endurance. Just like athletes need to fuel their bodies to train and compete, we need to fuel our spirits to stay strong in our faith. Life is filled with challenges, and there will be times when our faith is tested. It is in those moments that the sustenance from God's Word becomes even more important. When we have been regularly feeding on Scripture, we have a reservoir of strength to draw from, making it easier to stand firm in our beliefs and resist temptations or doubts. The Bible reminds us of God's promises, helping us stay focused on His truth rather than being swayed by fear or uncertainty. When we've been nourished by Scripture, we're better prepared to handle difficult situations with grace and patience, knowing that God's Word is alive within us, giving us the strength we need to persevere. This spiritual endurance is one of the most valuable benefits of being nourished by God's Word, as it helps us to remain faithful and hopeful, even when life feels overwhelming.

Feeding on Scripture daily also deepens our relationship with God. The Bible is a way for us to connect with Him, to hear His voice, and to understand His will for our lives. Spending time in the Word is like having a daily conversation with God, where we listen to His guidance, learn about His character, and open our hearts to His love and wisdom. This daily connection brings us closer to God, helping us to see His presence in every aspect of our lives. Just as sharing meals with friends or family strengthens our relationships with them, spending time in Scripture strengthens our relationship with God. We get to know Him better, understand His love for us, and grow in our desire to live according to His ways. This close connection to God is one of the greatest sources of peace and joy, as it fills our lives with purpose and helps us to feel secure, knowing that we are loved and guided by our Creator. When we feed on Scripture, we're not just reading words; we're building a relationship with God that gives our lives meaning and direction.

The Bible as sustenance also teaches us about the importance of balance in our spiritual diet. Just like our bodies need a variety of nutrients to stay healthy, our spirits benefit from a balanced approach to Scripture. The Bible offers many types of spiritual "food"—stories of faith, teachings about love and forgiveness, wisdom for making decisions, guidance on how to pray, and so much more. By reading different parts of the Bible, we get a full picture of God's plan and character, which strengthens every part of our spiritual life. If we only focus on one aspect, like reading only comforting verses, we might miss out on important lessons about growth, discipline, or serving others. A balanced approach to Scripture ensures that we are growing in all areas of our faith, not just the ones that feel easy or comfortable. This well-rounded spiritual diet keeps us strong, resilient, and prepared to face all aspects of life with a faith that is grounded in a deep understanding of God's truth.

Another important aspect of Scripture as sustenance is that it helps us to grow in wisdom and understanding. The Bible is filled with lessons about how to live a life that is pleasing to God, how to make wise choices, and how to treat others with kindness and respect. By reading and reflecting on these lessons, we gain insights that help us navigate our lives with integrity and grace. This wisdom is like food for our minds and hearts, shaping our thoughts and guiding our actions. As we continue to feed on God's Word, we become more discerning, better able to understand what is true and right. This growth in wisdom helps us make decisions that honor God and reflect His love to others. It also protects us from being led astray by false teachings or harmful influences, keeping us rooted in God's truth. The nourishment we gain from Scripture equips us to live lives that are full of purpose, compassion, and joy, reflecting the wisdom and love of God in everything we do.

Feeding on Scripture also helps us to experience peace and hope in times of trouble. Life is full of challenges, and there will be times when we feel anxious, afraid, or uncertain. During these moments, the Bible offers words of comfort and reassurance, reminding us that God is with us and that He is in control. Passages like Psalm 23, which speaks of God as our shepherd, provide a sense of peace that soothes our hearts and minds. These verses act like a calming meal for our spirit, giving us the sustenance we need to face difficult times with courage and trust. This peace is one of the greatest gifts of feeding on God's Word, as it helps us to remain calm and hopeful, even in the face of life's storms. By continually returning to Scripture, we are reminded of God's promises, His faithfulness, and His love, which strengthens us and helps us to find joy and gratitude in every season.

Lastly, the Bible as sustenance inspires us to serve and love others. When we are spiritually nourished by God's Word, we are filled with His love, compassion, and grace, which naturally flows out to those around us. Just as physical nourishment gives us the energy to work, help others, and be active, spiritual nourishment from Scripture gives us the strength and motivation to serve, encourage, and support those in need. It reminds us of our calling to be a light in the world, to love our neighbors, and to show kindness and generosity. This inspiration to serve is one of the ways that God's Word sustains not only our own spirits but also the lives of others. When we are rooted in Scripture, we are better able to share God's love, to offer encouragement, and to make a positive impact in the lives of those around us. Feeding on God's Word daily doesn't just change us; it changes the world around us, spreading love, hope, and kindness in ways that reflect God's character.

In conclusion, the Bible as a source of sustenance is a vital part of a strong and vibrant spiritual life. It provides the nourishment, wisdom, strength, and peace that we need to grow closer to God and to live lives that reflect His love and truth. By feeding on Scripture daily, we stay connected to God, build a deep and lasting relationship with Him, and are equipped to face life's challenges with faith, hope, and joy. This spiritual nourishment transforms us, strengthens us, and fills us with purpose, enabling us to live lives that honor God and bless those around us.

Chapter 12 - Soul-Revealing

The idea of Soul-Revealing through God's Word is one of the most profound aspects of Scripture, as it has the unique power to reach into our hearts and uncover who we truly are. When we say that the Bible reveals the "soul," we're talking about how it sheds light on our innermost emotions, thoughts, and desires—things that we might not even fully understand ourselves. It's almost as if God's Word is like a mirror for the soul, showing us both our strengths and our weaknesses, our hopes and our fears, our joys and our struggles. Scripture has this extraordinary ability to reflect back to us what's inside, helping us to see clearly what lies beneath the surface of our everyday lives. Our souls are made up of complex layers of feelings, ideas, and intentions that shape how we think, feel, and act. Often, these inner thoughts and emotions can be hard to sort through on our own, especially when they become tangled or overwhelming. But by turning to Scripture, we allow God's truth to guide us and bring clarity to our mental and emotional state. The Bible doesn't just skim the surface; it goes deep, reaching into those parts of us that may be hidden or overlooked. In doing so, it helps us to understand ourselves better, giving us insight into why we feel certain ways, why we react to situations the way we do, and how we can grow and change to become more aligned with God's will. This self-awareness is essential for personal growth and spiritual maturity, as it allows us to identify areas in our lives that need healing, adjustment, or strengthening.

One of the most remarkable things about the Bible's soul-revealing nature is that it speaks to us in a way that feels personal and specific, even though it was written thousands of years ago. No matter where we are in life—whether we're feeling happy, sad, anxious, or lost—Scripture has a way of reaching us right where we are. It's as though God knew exactly what we would need in every moment, and He provided words that can bring comfort, guidance, or conviction at just the right time. For example, when we're feeling weighed down by guilt or regret, verses about God's forgiveness can bring a sense of relief and peace. When we're feeling fearful, passages about God's protection and strength remind us that we are not alone. This ability to touch our hearts so deeply is what makes Scripture such a powerful tool for revealing the soul. It doesn't just give us information; it connects with us on a personal level, helping us to see ourselves as God sees us—fully known, deeply loved, and always valued.

The Bible's power to reveal the soul also means it helps us to see both the good and the not-so-good parts of ourselves. It celebrates our strengths, our potential, and the unique gifts that God has placed within us, reminding us that we are wonderfully made with a purpose. But it also points out areas where we might be struggling, where our thoughts or emotions may not align with God's truth. For example, we might read a verse that encourages kindness and realize that we've been holding onto bitterness or anger toward someone. Or we might come across a teaching about humility and realize that we've been acting out of pride or seeking approval from others instead of from God. This isn't meant to make us feel bad about ourselves; rather, it's an invitation to grow and to become more like Christ. By revealing these areas, Scripture guides us gently but firmly, helping us to let go of what doesn't belong and to embrace what does. It's a process of refinement and healing that brings us closer to the person God created us to be.

Turning to Scripture to gain insight into our mental and emotional state is incredibly helpful, especially in a world where so many influences can shape our thoughts and feelings. It's easy to get caught up in the pressures and expectations of society, or to be swayed by the opinions of others. But the Bible gives us a solid foundation, a true standard against which we can measure our thoughts and emotions. It helps us to discern what is truly good and right, giving us wisdom to separate God's truth from the lies or misconceptions we might hold about ourselves. For instance, we may struggle with feelings of worthlessness or insecurity, but the Bible reminds us that we are fearfully and wonderfully made, created in the image of God with a unique purpose. These truths help to reshape our self-image, replacing negative thoughts with God's perspective on who we are. This insight is incredibly freeing, as it allows us to let go of self-doubt and embrace our true identity as beloved children of God.

Another powerful aspect of Scripture as a soul-revealing tool is its ability to bring healing to our emotional wounds. Life can be tough, and many of us carry hurt, disappointment, or grief that we don't know how to deal with. These emotions can sometimes become buried within us, affecting our thoughts, actions, and relationships without us even realizing it. But when we spend time in God's Word, it has a way of bringing these hidden wounds to the surface, gently prompting us to face and address them. Passages that speak of God's love, His healing power, and His presence in times of trouble can provide comfort and reassurance, reminding us that we don't have to carry our burdens alone. God's Word is like a balm for the soul, soothing the pain and helping us to release our hurts into His care. This process of healing allows us to move forward with a sense of peace and wholeness, enabling us to experience life more fully and freely.

The Bible also reveals our souls by encouraging us to examine our motives and intentions. Sometimes, we might do the right thing on the outside, but our hearts may not be in the right place. We may give to others out of a sense of obligation rather than love, or we may seek success for the sake of pride rather than for God's glory. Scripture challenges us to look deeper, to question why we do what we do, and to align our actions with genuine love and humility. This type of self-reflection is crucial for spiritual growth, as it helps us to live with integrity and authenticity. By revealing our true motives, the Bible helps us to become more honest with ourselves and with God, leading to a more genuine and meaningful faith. It's a call to live not just by actions, but by a heart that seeks to honor God in all things.

In addition to revealing our own thoughts and emotions, the Bible also helps us to understand the nature of our relationships with others. It teaches us about forgiveness, compassion, patience, and love, qualities that are essential for healthy, fulfilling relationships. By examining ourselves in the light of Scripture, we can see where we may need to grow in these areas. Perhaps we struggle with forgiveness, holding onto grudges that keep us from experiencing peace. Or maybe we find it difficult to show compassion to those who are different from us. The Bible provides guidance on how to overcome these challenges, encouraging us to let go of resentment, to extend grace, and to love others as Christ loves us. This insight into our relationships is a gift, as it helps us to build stronger, more loving connections with the people in our lives, reflecting God's love in all that we do.

Ultimately, the Bible's role as a soul-revealer is about bringing us closer to God and to His purpose for our lives. By exposing our true thoughts, emotions, and desires, it invites us into a deeper relationship with Him, one that is built on honesty, trust, and love. When we allow Scripture to reveal our souls, we are opening ourselves up to a transformative journey of faith, one that changes us from the inside out. It's not always easy, as it often requires us to face uncomfortable truths or to let go of things we've held onto for too long. But this process of self-discovery and growth is worth it, as it leads us to a life that is more aligned with God's will, filled with peace, joy, and purpose. Through the soul-revealing power of God's Word, we come to see ourselves more clearly, to understand our strengths and weaknesses, and to embrace the incredible potential that God has placed within us. This journey of self-discovery is a lifelong process, but it is one that brings us ever closer to the heart of God, transforming us into the people He created us to be.

Chapter 13 - Standard of Truth

The concept of God's Word as the Standard of Truth is incredibly important because it provides us with a solid foundation in a world filled with confusing messages, changing opinions, and conflicting values. The Bible describes itself as "quick and powerful," which means it's alive and active, having the strength to cut through the noise and reach directly to the heart of what is real, right, and true. In a world where everyone seems to have their own version of truth, and where beliefs can shift based on trends, personal opinions, or cultural pressures, the Bible remains an unchanging standard we can rely on. God's Word isn't just a book of good ideas or moral guidelines; it is the ultimate measure of truth, giving us a clear, dependable, and eternal perspective on what is right and wrong. When we hold everything we hear, see, or believe up against Scripture, we can discern what is actually true from what might simply be appealing, popular, or even misleading. The Bible acts like a compass for our lives, pointing us consistently toward God's ways, no matter how the world around us changes. This truth is both comforting and empowering because it means we don't have to be swayed by every new idea or pressured into accepting beliefs that go against God's design. Instead, we have a reliable source that grounds us, helping us stay steady, focused, and confident in our faith.

Using the Bible as our standard of truth means that it becomes our go-to source for guidance and wisdom in all areas of life. Whenever we face a decision, whether it's about relationships, our career, how we handle our finances, or how we treat others, we can look to Scripture to understand what God's principles are. It gives us a clear framework for living a life that honors Him, and it shows us what values truly matter. For example, while the world might tell us that success is all about wealth or status, the Bible teaches us that true success comes from loving God, serving others, and living with integrity and humility. This standard of truth helps us to prioritize the right things, focusing on what is eternal rather than getting caught up in temporary achievements. God's Word reminds us that our worth is not based on outward success or appearance but on our relationship with Him and our obedience to His ways. This perspective is freeing because it releases us from the pressures of trying to meet society's ever-changing expectations, allowing us to live in a way that pleases God and brings us true fulfillment.

Another powerful aspect of the Bible as the standard of truth is that it helps us to identify and resist deception. In today's world, it's easy to be influenced by messages that may sound good but are not truly aligned with God's truth. These messages can come from media, friends, social media, or even our own thoughts. But when we hold these ideas up against Scripture, we can see whether they align with God's Word or not. The Bible serves as a filter, helping us to sort out what is true from what is false. For instance, the world might encourage us to prioritize self-interest, but the Bible teaches us to love others selflessly. By comparing these messages to Scripture, we can avoid being led astray by beliefs that may seem attractive but ultimately don't bring us closer to God. This discernment is essential for maintaining a healthy and strong faith because it keeps us rooted in God's ways, rather than being pulled in every direction by the latest trend or opinion. The Bible's truth doesn't change, so we can trust that it will guide us consistently, providing clarity and direction in a confusing world.

Holding everything we hear or believe against the standard of Scripture also strengthens our relationship with God. When we turn to the Bible for answers and direction, we are choosing to trust in God's wisdom rather than relying solely on our own understanding. This choice to lean on God's truth deepens our faith, helping us to build a life that is centered on His Word. The Bible shows us not only what is true but also why it matters, revealing God's heart and His desires for us. By aligning our lives with Scripture, we begin to see the world through God's perspective, understanding the deeper meaning behind His commandments and the purpose He has for each of us. This connection to God's truth brings peace and assurance, especially when we face difficult situations or challenges. Instead of feeling lost or unsure, we can rest in the knowledge that God's Word is guiding us, lighting our path and giving us the strength to make choices that honor Him. This sense of purpose and direction is one of the most fulfilling aspects of living by God's standard of truth, as it fills our lives with meaning and helps us to navigate life's ups and downs with confidence.

Applying Scripture as our standard of truth also encourages personal growth and self-reflection. The Bible doesn't just show us what's wrong in the world; it also helps us to examine our own hearts, thoughts, and actions. It challenges us to live by higher standards, encouraging us to grow in kindness, patience, humility, and love. By regularly reading and reflecting on Scripture, we allow it to shape our character, helping us to become more Christ-like in everything we do. This transformation is a lifelong process, but it is one that brings us closer to God and makes a positive impact on those around us. As we become more grounded in God's truth, we develop the strength and courage to stand up for what is right, even when it's difficult or unpopular. We learn to speak the truth in love, to act with integrity, and to treat others with respect and compassion. These qualities not only benefit us but also serve as a testimony to others, showing the world the difference that living by God's truth can make.

In a world where truth often feels relative and subjective, the Bible offers a firm foundation that doesn't shift or change. God's Word has stood the test of time, proving itself to be reliable, trustworthy, and relevant across generations. This timeless truth is something we can build our lives upon, knowing that it will never fail us. While society's values and morals may shift over time, the principles in Scripture remain constant, providing us with a clear and steady guide for how to live. This stability is comforting, as it gives us a sense of security in a world that is often chaotic and unpredictable. No matter what changes may come, we know that God's Word is a rock we can rely on, giving us the stability we need to live with purpose and confidence.

Ultimately, holding everything up to the standard of Scripture helps us to become people who reflect God's love, truth, and grace to the world. By living according to His Word, we become lights in a world that is often filled with darkness and confusion. Our lives become a reflection of God's truth, showing others the peace, joy, and strength that come from a relationship with Him. This impact goes beyond our own personal growth; it has the power to influence those around us, inspiring others to seek God's truth for themselves. In this way, the Bible's role as the standard of truth not only transforms our own lives but also has a ripple effect, spreading God's love and truth to others. By staying rooted in Scripture, we are equipped to face life's challenges, to resist deception, and to live with integrity, making a lasting difference in the world around us.

Chapter 14 - Sword of the Spirit

The Sword of the Spirit, which is God's Word, is one of the most powerful tools we have for facing life's challenges and standing strong in our faith. The Bible describes it as being sharper than any sword, meaning it can cut through confusion, lies, and doubts, going straight to the heart of what's true and what's real. When we think of a sword, we picture a weapon that is used in battle, something that protects and defends but can also strike with strength and precision. That's exactly what Scripture does for us in our spiritual battles—it becomes our weapon to defend ourselves against negativity, temptations, and fears that try to pull us away from God. Life is full of challenges, both big and small, and many of these challenges are not just physical or emotional but are spiritual at their core. These are battles that we can't see, struggles within our minds, our hearts, and our spirits, where we face doubts, fear, guilt, and sometimes even a sense of hopelessness. When we use God's Word as the Sword of the Spirit, we're equipping ourselves with a weapon that can overcome these invisible battles, helping us to stand firm in our faith and to walk confidently in the path God has set for us. Just as a soldier would never enter a battlefield without a sword, we shouldn't go through life without the strength and guidance that comes from Scripture.

Using the Bible as our spiritual weapon means we can defend ourselves when we feel attacked by things that try to shake our faith. For example, when we face doubts or feelings of insecurity, the Word reminds us of God's promises, telling us that we are loved, chosen, and valuable in His eyes. Verses like "I can do all things through Christ who strengthens me" (Philippians 4:13) become our shield, blocking out thoughts that try to make us feel weak or unworthy. When we're tempted to do something that we know isn't right, Scripture acts like a sword, cutting through the temptation and giving us the courage to choose what's right. Just like Jesus used Scripture to resist the devil's temptations in the wilderness, we too can use the Word to resist temptations that try to pull us away from God's path. Each verse becomes a powerful reminder of God's truth, giving us the strength to stand firm. This is what makes the Bible not just a book, but a living, active tool that helps us in real, practical ways every day.

The Sword of the Spirit is not only for defense; it's also an offensive weapon. When we use Scripture actively, we're not just waiting to respond to problems; we're taking steps to grow stronger and deepen our faith. By regularly reading and studying the Bible, we build up our knowledge of God's truth, making us more prepared and resilient. This knowledge of Scripture is like practicing with a sword so that when battles come, we're ready to respond confidently. When doubts arise, or when people question our beliefs, we can use the Word to speak truth boldly and to clarify what we know is real and good. Scripture gives us the courage to share our faith, to stand up for what's right, and to help others find their way to God. By using the Bible as our Sword of the Spirit, we become warriors for God's kingdom, ready to face challenges and make a positive impact on the world around us. Each time we share a verse with someone who needs encouragement or stand firm in a difficult situation because of a Bible verse we've held onto, we're using Scripture as an offensive tool, pushing back darkness and spreading God's light.

The power of the Sword of the Spirit is that it connects us directly to God's strength and wisdom. Unlike earthly weapons that can be blunt or break over time, God's Word never loses its power. It is always effective, always sharp, and always ready to help us, no matter how challenging the situation may be. This is because Scripture is filled with God's truth, wisdom, and promises, which are eternal and unchanging. When we hold onto a verse or passage, it's like holding onto a piece of God's strength. This strength is especially important in times of spiritual struggle, when we feel weak or unsure. By remembering God's promises and letting them guide our actions, we are empowered to overcome anything that comes our way. It's not our own strength that wins the battle; it's God's strength working through His Word. This reliance on Scripture doesn't make us passive; it makes us active and prepared, giving us confidence that we can face any spiritual challenge with courage and faith.

Scripture as the Sword of the Spirit also has the power to bring peace and clarity in times of confusion or fear. Life is often filled with moments where we feel unsure or scared, but the Bible cuts through these fears with truth and reassurance. When we're worried about the future, verses about God's faithfulness remind us that He is in control and has good plans for us. When we're overwhelmed by guilt, verses about forgiveness reassure us that we are redeemed and loved by God. Each verse becomes like a lifeline, pulling us out of fear and grounding us in peace. This is why it's so important to spend time in God's Word regularly; the more we know Scripture, the more prepared we are to use it as our weapon in times of need. Just as a soldier practices and trains with their sword, we too should be familiar with the Bible, knowing where to find verses that bring us strength and peace. This familiarity with Scripture makes it easier to turn to God's Word whenever we face a battle, allowing us to respond quickly and effectively.

In addition to personal battles, the Sword of the Spirit equips us to help others in their struggles. When friends, family, or even strangers are going through tough times, we can use Scripture to offer them comfort, encouragement, and hope. Sharing a verse or a story from the Bible can be a powerful way to remind others of God's presence and His love. This not only helps them but also strengthens our own faith, as it reminds us of the power and truth of God's Word. Each time we use Scripture to support others, we're engaging in spiritual warfare on their behalf, helping them to stand strong and reminding them that they're not alone. This act of sharing God's Word makes the Bible not just a personal weapon but a tool for building up the faith of others, creating a community of believers who are united in God's truth and strength.

Ultimately, the Sword of the Spirit is about standing firm in our faith and living a life that reflects God's love and truth. By using Scripture as our weapon, we protect ourselves from being swayed by false teachings, negativity, and anything that tries to pull us away from God. We become grounded in God's truth, equipped to resist anything that goes against His Word, and able to boldly live out our faith in a way that honors Him. This doesn't mean life will be without challenges, but it does mean that we'll be prepared to face them with confidence, knowing that we have God's Word as our weapon and our guide. The Sword of the Spirit is a gift from God, given to help us navigate life's battles and to remain faithful, strong, and courageous in our walk with Him.

Chapter 15 - Strengthens Faith

The idea that God's Word Strengthens Faith is incredibly powerful because it means that the Bible has the unique ability to grow, deepen, and reinforce our belief in God and His promises. Faith is one of the most important aspects of our spiritual lives, as it shapes how we see the world, how we respond to challenges, and how we relate to God. But faith isn't always something that comes easily, especially when we're faced with tough situations, doubts, or fears. This is why Scripture is so vital—it is a living, active force that has the power to feed and empower our faith, making it stronger day by day. Just as food nourishes our bodies, the Word of God nourishes our souls, giving us the strength to trust in God's love, wisdom, and power even when things don't make sense or when we're struggling. The Bible isn't just a collection of stories or teachings; it is alive with God's Spirit, filled with truths that speak directly to our hearts and remind us of who God is and what He has done. When we meditate on Scripture, we're not just reading words; we're allowing those words to sink into our minds and souls, building a foundation of trust in God that becomes unshakable over time.

The Bible strengthens our faith by reminding us of God's promises, His character, and His mighty works. Throughout Scripture, we see example after example of God's faithfulness to His people—stories of deliverance, healing, provision, and protection that show us that God is always present and always trustworthy. When we read about how God parted the Red Sea to save the Israelites, healed the sick, and provided for those in need, it strengthens our belief that He can do the same for us. These stories serve as a reminder that God is the same yesterday, today, and forever, meaning that the same God who performed miracles in the Bible is still at work in our lives today. This knowledge gives us confidence, knowing that we are not alone and that God's power is greater than any obstacle we might face. Each time we read a story of

God's faithfulness, it's like adding another brick to the foundation of our faith, making it stronger and more secure.

Scripture also strengthens our faith by giving us wisdom and guidance for the challenges we face. Life is full of situations that can make us feel uncertain or afraid, whether it's dealing with loss, facing a difficult decision, or going through a time of change. The Bible provides a source of wisdom that helps us navigate these situations with faith rather than fear. Verses like "Trust in the Lord with all your heart and lean not on your own understanding" (Proverbs 3:5) remind us to rely on God's guidance, even when we don't have all the answers. This kind of wisdom gives us the courage to move forward, knowing that we can trust God's plan for us. When we meditate on these verses, they become a part of us, giving us strength and reassurance when we need it most. This wisdom from Scripture is like a roadmap that shows us the way forward, helping us to make decisions that are grounded in faith and aligned with God's will.

One of the most beautiful things about how Scripture strengthens faith is that it meets us exactly where we are. Whether we are full of faith or struggling with doubts, God's Word speaks to us personally and directly, addressing our needs and concerns. For those who feel weak in their faith, the Bible offers encouragement, reminding us that even a small amount of faith can move mountains. For those who feel strong, it provides reminders of humility and trust, encouraging us to keep our eyes on God rather than on our own abilities. This adaptability makes Scripture a constant source of strength, no matter what we're going through. When we feel like we're barely hanging on, verses about God's love and support lift us up. When we feel confident, verses about relying on God keep us grounded. In every situation, the Bible has something to say that can bolster our faith, helping us to stay connected to God and to grow stronger in our trust in Him.

Another way Scripture empowers faith is by helping us to see beyond our immediate circumstances. Sometimes, life can feel overwhelming, and it's easy to get caught up in the problems right in front of us. But the Bible reminds us that there is a bigger picture, one that is filled with God's promises for the future. Verses about eternal life, God's kingdom, and His plans for us remind us that our current struggles are only temporary and that God has a greater purpose for our lives. This perspective helps us to hold onto hope, even when things are tough, because we know that God is working all things for our good. Meditating on these promises fills us with hope and strengthens our faith, reminding us that we are part of a story that is bigger than ourselves. This hope gives us the endurance to keep going, to trust in God's timing, and to believe that He is working even when we can't see it.

The Bible also strengthens our faith by teaching us about God's character. The more we read Scripture, the more we learn about who God is—His love, His justice, His mercy, and His faithfulness. These attributes of God are not just ideas; they are realities that affect how we live and how we trust in Him. When we understand that God is always good, that He never fails, and that He loves us unconditionally, it becomes easier to place our faith in Him, no matter what happens. Knowing God's character gives us a foundation that is unshakable, because we know that our faith is not based on circumstances but on a God who is trustworthy and true. This understanding of God's character deepens our faith, helping us to trust Him more fully and to rely on His promises even when life is uncertain.

Meditating on Scripture as a way to strengthen faith is a practice that brings incredible benefits over time. By spending regular time in God's Word, we allow His truths to sink into our hearts and minds, building a faith that is resilient and steadfast. Meditation is not just about reading; it's about reflecting, praying, and letting God's Word shape our thoughts and beliefs. This practice helps us to internalize Scripture, so that it becomes a part of us, ready to strengthen us whenever we need it. Just as an athlete trains their muscles through regular exercise, we strengthen our faith through the regular "exercise" of meditating on God's Word. This continual focus on Scripture fills us with God's wisdom and strength, equipping us to face challenges with confidence and peace.

In conclusion, the Bible as a strengthener of faith is one of the most valuable gifts we have. It empowers us, fortifies our trust in God, and gives us the courage to walk through life with hope and confidence. By meditating on Scripture, we build a faith that is strong, resilient, and deeply rooted in God's truth. This faith not only sustains us in times of trouble but also brings us closer to God, helping us to experience His love, guidance, and peace in a powerful way. Through God's Word, our faith is made strong, enabling us to live fully and faithfully as we follow Him.

Chapter 16 – Stability

The concept of Stability in life through God's Word is one of the most valuable gifts for anyone facing the ups and downs of life. The Bible acts as a solid anchor that keeps us grounded, balanced, and secure, no matter what we go through. Life is full of changes, unexpected situations, and difficult moments that can feel overwhelming. We may face times of uncertainty, challenges at work, struggles in relationships, or even internal battles within ourselves. Without something steady to hold onto, we can easily feel tossed around by our emotions, circumstances, or the opinions of others. But God's Word gives us stability; it is the unchanging truth in a world where almost everything else is temporary and unpredictable. When we turn to the Bible, we are reminded of God's promises, His love, and His wisdom, which are always there to guide us and give us a sense of peace and security. It's like having a foundation that we can build our lives upon, knowing it won't shake or crumble when things get hard. No matter how strong the winds of change blow, the Bible remains firm, keeping us steady and helping us to stay focused on what truly matters.

The stability that comes from Scripture is unique because it doesn't rely on anything temporary, like success, money, or popularity, which can all change in an instant. Instead, the Bible grounds us in eternal truths—things that are always true and reliable because they come from God. For instance, it teaches us about God's faithfulness, showing us that He is always with us and that He never changes. When we know that God's love for us is constant and unchanging, it gives us a sense of stability that nothing else can provide. We don't have to worry about earning His love or fear that it will be taken away; instead, we can rest in the assurance that God's love is a steady presence in our lives. This knowledge gives us a kind of balance and confidence that helps us face each day with peace, knowing that we are loved and cared for by our

Creator. In a world that often feels unstable, God's Word provides a secure place to turn, giving us the strength and courage to stand firm.

Another way that Scripture brings stability is by offering guidance for making wise decisions. Life is filled with choices, and sometimes it's hard to know what the right path is. The Bible serves as a roadmap, showing us the way to live a life that honors God and brings us peace and fulfillment. It teaches us principles like honesty, kindness, patience, and humility, which help us to make decisions that are in line with God's will. By following these principles, we create a life that is balanced and stable, avoiding the chaos that often comes from poor choices or impulsive actions. For example, if we are tempted to act out of anger or selfishness, Scripture reminds us to respond with love and patience instead. This guidance keeps us from making decisions that we might later regret, allowing us to live in a way that is peaceful and centered. Each time we make a choice that aligns with God's Word, we build a stronger foundation for our lives, creating stability that helps us to weather any storm.

In addition to guiding our decisions, the Bible also helps us to understand and manage our emotions. Emotions are a natural part of life, and they can be wonderful, but they can also lead us astray if we aren't careful. Feelings like fear, anger, jealousy, and sadness can sometimes take over, making us feel unbalanced or overwhelmed. But Scripture gives us a way to process and understand these emotions, reminding us that we don't have to be controlled by them. For example, when we feel anxious or afraid, verses about God's peace and protection can calm our hearts and help us to trust in Him. When we're angry, the Bible reminds us to forgive and let go of resentment, which keeps us from being weighed down by bitterness. By grounding our emotions in God's truth, we find a stability that allows us to handle life's ups and downs with grace. Instead of being swayed by every feeling, we learn to stay rooted in God's promises, which bring a sense of calm and balance no matter what we're facing.

The stability that God's Word provides is also important in times of trouble or crisis. When life is difficult—whether due to loss, disappointment, illness, or any other challenge—it's easy to feel shaken. During these times, we need something firm to hold onto, something that will keep us steady when everything else seems uncertain. The Bible offers this stability by reminding us of God's presence, His power, and His love. It tells us that God is our refuge, a strong tower in times of trouble, and that He will never leave us nor forsake us. These promises give us the courage to face hardship with faith, knowing that we are not alone and that God is with us every step of the way. This sense of stability doesn't mean that we won't feel sadness or fear, but it means that we can hold onto hope even in the darkest moments, trusting that God is in control and that He is working all things for our good.

Letting God's Word be our anchor means that we continually return to it for strength, comfort, and direction. Just as a ship needs an anchor to stay grounded in the water, we need Scripture to keep us grounded in life. This means making a habit of reading, studying, and reflecting on the Bible regularly, so that its truths are always fresh in our minds. By doing this, we build a strong foundation of faith that becomes our steady support in both good times and bad. This regular connection to Scripture helps us to stay focused on God's promises and to remember what truly matters, keeping us from being distracted or discouraged by temporary struggles. It's like having a steady hand to guide us, reminding us of God's faithfulness and helping us to remain calm and focused no matter what comes our way.

The stability we gain from Scripture also positively impacts our relationships. When we are grounded in God's truth, we are better able to show love, patience, and forgiveness to others, creating stronger and healthier connections. We are less likely to react out of anger or selfishness because we are guided by God's wisdom, which encourages us to treat others with respect and kindness. This stability allows us to be a source of support and encouragement to those around us, sharing God's love and helping others to find peace as well. By building our lives on the stable foundation of God's Word, we create an environment where our relationships can thrive, bringing harmony and joy to our families, friendships, and communities.

Ultimately, the stability that comes from God's Word is about building a life that is rooted in faith, hope, and love. It's about knowing who we are in Christ and being confident in His love and His plans for us. This stability allows us to face the future with courage, to handle challenges with grace, and to live each day with a sense of peace that comes from trusting in God's unchanging Word. By letting the Bible be our anchor, we find a strength and stability that no storm can shake, enabling us to live a life that reflects God's goodness and brings glory to Him in all that we do.

Chapter 17 - Spiritual Growth

The concept of Spiritual Growth through God's Word is one of the most essential aspects of the Christian journey, as it is both powerful and life-giving, promoting continual growth in faith and helping believers become spiritually mature. Spiritual growth is a lifelong process that requires commitment, dedication, and a heart open to change. It's about becoming more like Christ each day, learning to walk in love, grace, patience, and wisdom. God's Word acts as the fuel for this growth, giving us the knowledge, encouragement, and guidance we need to develop a deep, meaningful relationship with God. The Bible isn't just a book we read; it's a living document filled with truths that speak directly to our hearts, helping us to understand God's character, His promises, and His purposes for our lives. Every time we study Scripture, it's like planting seeds in our hearts that grow into qualities like faith, kindness, and understanding. Just as plants need sunlight, water, and soil to grow, our spirits need the nourishment of God's Word to thrive. Without it, our spiritual lives can become stagnant, weak, or easily shaken by life's challenges. But with regular study and reflection on Scripture, we find ourselves rooted in God's truth, growing stronger and more resilient with each passing day.

One of the most powerful ways that the Bible promotes spiritual growth is by teaching us about God's nature and His love for us. Through stories, teachings, and parables, we learn that God is faithful, just, merciful, and ever-present. This understanding builds our faith, helping us to trust Him more deeply, even when we can't see the full picture. Knowing that God's love is constant and that His plans for us are good provides a solid foundation that encourages growth. The more we study Scripture, the more we recognize that our relationship with God is not based on our performance but on His grace. This knowledge frees us from fear and insecurity, allowing us to grow confidently in our faith, knowing that we are loved and accepted by God. Each passage we read reminds us of who God is and who we are in Him, providing the assurance and motivation we need to keep growing and maturing in our spiritual walk.

Scripture also promotes growth by challenging us to examine our hearts, actions, and attitudes. The Bible acts as a mirror, reflecting areas in our lives where we may need to change or improve. For instance, we may read verses that encourage forgiveness and realize that we're holding onto bitterness, or we may come across teachings on humility and recognize that we've been acting out of pride. These moments of self-reflection are not meant to make us feel guilty but to guide us toward a better way of living. By showing us where we fall short, the Bible gives us the opportunity to grow in character and to align our lives more closely with God's will. This process of self-examination is essential for spiritual growth, as it helps us to shed behaviors, thoughts, and attitudes that hold us back, making room for qualities like love, patience, and kindness to take root in our hearts.

Another important aspect of spiritual growth through Scripture is the wisdom and guidance it provides for everyday life. Life is filled with choices, challenges, and moments of uncertainty, and the Bible offers a clear path to follow. It provides principles for how to handle relationships, manage our resources, deal with stress, and make decisions that honor God. By studying Scripture, we gain insights into God's wisdom, which helps us to navigate life's ups and downs with confidence and peace. This guidance is not only about knowing what to do but about developing a mindset and a heart that are in tune with God's will. Over time, as we apply these teachings, we grow in spiritual maturity, becoming people who make choices that reflect our faith and who live in a way that honors God. This wisdom from Scripture is like a compass that keeps us on the right path, helping us to grow steadily in our relationship with God and in our understanding of what it means to live a life that reflects His love and truth.

Spiritual growth through God's Word also involves developing resilience and strength to face challenges. The Bible doesn't promise a life free from difficulties, but it does equip us with the faith and courage to overcome them. Passages about perseverance, trust, and hope remind us that God is with us in every trial, providing the strength we need to endure. By meditating on these verses, we build up our inner strength, allowing us to face hardships without losing faith. This resilience is a key aspect of spiritual maturity, as it helps us to remain steady and grounded, even when life feels uncertain or overwhelming. The more we study Scripture, the more prepared we become to handle adversity with grace and trust, knowing that our foundation is rooted in God's promises. This steady growth makes us less likely to be shaken by fear or doubt, giving us the courage to move forward with confidence, even in difficult times.

Another way that Scripture promotes spiritual growth is by teaching us how to love others. The Bible is filled with teachings on kindness, forgiveness, compassion, and humility—qualities that are essential for building strong, healthy relationships. As we study these teachings and apply them to our lives, we learn to treat others with respect and understanding, even when it's challenging. This growth in love is a fundamental part of spiritual maturity, as it reflects the heart of God and shows the world His love through our actions. By growing in our ability to love others, we become more like Christ, who demonstrated the ultimate example of love and sacrifice. This transformation in how we treat others not only strengthens our relationships but also deepens our connection with God, as we learn to see others through His eyes and to act with compassion and grace in all we do.

The Bible also helps us grow spiritually by teaching us to rely on God rather than on our own understanding. Life is often unpredictable, and there are times when we may not understand why certain things happen. Scripture reminds us that God's ways are higher than ours and that His plans for us are good, even when we can't see the full picture. This trust in God's sovereignty is a key aspect of spiritual growth, as it teaches us to let go of control and to place our faith in Him. By learning to rely on God, we develop a peace that goes beyond our circumstances, knowing that He is guiding our steps and that His love is always with us. This trust allows us to grow in patience and faith, helping us to wait on God's timing and to embrace His will, even when it doesn't align with our own plans.

Studying God's Word also encourages growth by filling us with hope and joy. The Bible is filled with promises of God's love, His presence, and His future plans for us, which fill our hearts with hope. This hope is a powerful force that fuels our growth, reminding us that we have a purpose and that our lives are part of a greater story. When we meditate on these promises, we are filled with a sense of joy and gratitude, even in challenging times. This joy is not based on our circumstances but on the knowledge that we are loved by God and that He has a plan for our lives. This perspective brings a sense of peace and contentment that strengthens our faith and allows us to face each day with a positive attitude. As we grow in our understanding of God's promises, we become more joyful, hopeful, and resilient, qualities that are essential for a strong and mature faith.

In conclusion, the Bible as a source of spiritual growth is a powerful and life-giving tool that promotes continual growth in faith. By studying Scripture, we are transformed from the inside out, becoming more like Christ and developing qualities that reflect God's love and truth. This growth is a lifelong journey, one that brings us closer to God and fills our lives with peace, joy, and purpose. Through God's Word, we gain wisdom, strength, resilience, and a deeper understanding of who we are in Him. This spiritual maturity not only benefits our own lives but also allows us to make a positive impact on those around us, sharing God's love and light in all that we do.

Chapter 18 – Sensitivity

The concept of Sensitivity developed through God's Word is incredibly important, as it gives us a way to become finely tuned to God's will and guidance. The Bible tells us that Scripture can discern the heart's thoughts, reaching deep within us to uncover things we might not even know about ourselves. This sensitivity is what allows us to grow closer to God, as it makes us more aware of His voice, His direction, and His desires for our lives. Just as a musician tunes an instrument to make it play beautiful, clear notes, God's Word helps us "tune" our hearts and minds to recognize what is from Him and what isn't. This process of becoming sensitive to God's guidance means we are no longer just going through life on our own terms but are actively listening for His lead. By developing this sensitivity, we learn to distinguish between our own desires and God's purpose for us, allowing us to follow His path rather than our own. When we study Scripture and meditate on its truths, we become more attuned to God's gentle nudges and corrections. It's like training our spiritual ears to pick up on God's frequency, helping us to hear His voice even amidst the noise of everyday life.

God's Word acts as a filter for our thoughts and intentions, helping us discern the purity and alignment of our heart's desires with God's will. This sensitivity brings us a deeper awareness of what is right and wrong in God's eyes, allowing us to make choices that reflect His character and honor His principles. When we encounter situations that challenge our integrity or tempt us to compromise our values, our God-attuned conscience, sharpened by Scripture, steps in to guide us toward what is righteous and pleasing to Him. This sensitivity keeps us from being led astray by the pressures and influences around us, grounding us in God's truth so that we don't compromise on what truly matters. By regularly spending time in the Word, we strengthen this ability to discern, learning to respond quickly and confidently to God's direction, and moving away from paths that would harm our relationship with Him. The more we listen to Scripture, the more we develop a moral compass that reflects God's heart, leading us to live with a sense of peace, purpose, and integrity in every aspect of life.

The sensitivity that God's Word builds in us is not only about moral choices but also about understanding and responding to God's personal guidance in our daily lives. When we are sensitive to God's voice, we are able to pick up on the ways He is speaking to us through circumstances, people, or even subtle inner promptings. For instance, we might feel an urge to reach out to someone who is struggling, or we might feel a sense of peace about a decision that aligns with God's Word. This sensitivity helps us to recognize these moments as God's gentle guidance, nudging us in a direction that brings us closer to His purpose. It's a bit like having an internal GPS that guides us through life's choices, relationships, and challenges, always pointing us back to God's will. The Bible teaches us to trust these inner promptings when they align with Scripture, giving us confidence to act in faith and to follow where God is leading. By cultivating this sensitivity, we become more open to God's plans and more willing to step out in obedience, knowing that we are walking in His wisdom and protection.

Sensitivity to God's will through Scripture also helps us navigate difficult emotions and situations with grace and discernment. Life often brings moments of anger, sadness, or frustration that can cloud our judgment and pull us away from God's peace. But when we are sensitive to God's guidance, we learn to respond to these emotions in ways that reflect His love and wisdom. For example, when faced with anger, Scripture reminds us to be "slow to anger and quick to forgive," helping us to release bitterness and seek reconciliation instead. When we are feeling anxious or afraid, verses about God's peace and protection help us to find comfort and strength. This sensitivity allows us to handle life's challenges with a spirit of calm and trust, rather than being swept away by our feelings. By turning to God's Word in these moments, we gain the clarity and self-control needed to respond in ways that honor God, building stronger, healthier relationships and creating an atmosphere of peace around us.

Another powerful aspect of sensitivity to God's Word is the compassion it brings to our relationships. As we grow more sensitive to God's voice, we become more aware of the needs and feelings of those around us. This empathy leads us to act with kindness, patience, and understanding, reflecting God's love in all our interactions. When we are sensitive to God's heart, we see others through His eyes, recognizing their struggles, pain, and hopes. This awareness encourages us to reach out, offer encouragement, or simply be present for those who need support. Scripture guides us to bear each other's burdens, to forgive, and to build each other up, and this sensitivity to God's Word enables us to live out these commands in real, tangible ways. By becoming more sensitive to God's guidance, we develop a spirit of compassion that transforms our relationships, making us agents of God's love and grace in a world that often lacks empathy.

This sensitivity also brings a deepened prayer life, as we become more aware of how God is working in and around us. When we listen to Scripture, we become more mindful of the ways we need to pray for ourselves and others. Our prayers become more aligned with God's heart, asking not just for what we want but for what brings Him glory and fulfills His purpose. This shift in our prayers reflects a growing maturity in our faith, as we seek to honor God's will above our own desires. The sensitivity developed through Scripture brings a sense of closeness to God in prayer, as we learn to listen as much as we speak, allowing God to shape our requests and guide our hearts. Our prayer life becomes richer, deeper, and more meaningful, filled with moments of reflection, gratitude, and the quiet assurance that God is near.

Finally, the sensitivity that Scripture builds in us is essential for spiritual growth and maturity. As we become more attuned to God's voice, we gain a clearer understanding of His purpose for our lives and a stronger commitment to live in a way that honors Him. This sensitivity is not just a skill; it is a relationship with God that grows over time, one that brings us closer to Him and transforms every part of our lives. By letting God's Word shape our thoughts, actions, and attitudes, we develop a faith that is grounded in God's truth and responsive to His leading. This sensitivity allows us to live a life that is fully connected to God, filled with His peace, love, and guidance, making every moment an opportunity to reflect His grace and purpose to the world around us.

Chapter 19 - Searches Our Heart

The idea that God's Word Searches Our Heart is one of the most profound and powerful aspects of Scripture because it goes beyond merely teaching us rules or giving us encouragement; it actually reaches deep within us to reveal the thoughts and intents that lie hidden in our hearts. The Bible is described as living and active, and when we read it with an open heart, it acts like a mirror that reflects who we truly are beneath the surface. God's Word has the unique ability to cut through our outer layers—our words, actions, and even our self-made identities—and go directly to the hidden parts of us that even we might not fully understand. These are the places where we hold our true desires, fears, motivations, and struggles, often tucked away from others and sometimes even from ourselves. The Word exposes these areas, not to shame or judge us, but to guide us toward growth, healing, and a closer relationship with God. By searching our hearts, Scripture helps us confront both our strengths and weaknesses, showing us where we're doing well and where we may need to change. This process can be uncomfortable because it requires honesty and humility, but it's also incredibly freeing and transformative. When we invite God to use His Word to reveal areas in our lives that need growth or change, we're allowing Him to shape us into people who reflect His love, grace, and truth more fully.

One of the most impactful ways that Scripture searches our hearts is by revealing our true intentions. Sometimes, we may believe we're acting out of kindness, generosity, or righteousness, but God's Word helps us look deeper to examine our motives. For instance, we may be generous, but if we're doing it to gain approval or praise, the Bible helps us see this and realign our actions with a purer heart. Or, we may serve others, but if we're doing it out of obligation rather than love, God's Word gently reveals this, prompting us to serve with genuine compassion. By exposing these hidden intentions, Scripture guides us toward a more sincere and authentic faith, encouraging us to live with integrity and a heart that genuinely seeks to honor God. This honesty with ourselves is essential for spiritual growth, as it allows us to identify areas where we may need to let go of pride, fear, or selfishness. By allowing the Bible to search our hearts, we are inviting God to transform us from within, creating a foundation of humility, sincerity, and love that strengthens our relationship with Him and with others.

The Bible's ability to search our hearts also helps us confront and address any hidden sins or habits that may be hindering our spiritual journey. Sometimes, we may hold onto things like bitterness, jealousy, or resentment without fully realizing how they're affecting us. These hidden sins can create barriers between us and God, as well as between us and others. But when we read Scripture, it reveals these things to us, showing us the impact they're having on our lives and encouraging us to let go of anything that doesn't align with God's will. For example, a verse about forgiveness may prompt us to forgive someone we've been holding a grudge against, or a teaching about humility may help us recognize areas where pride has crept into our hearts. This exposure isn't meant to make us feel guilty or ashamed; instead, it's an invitation to bring these issues to God and to seek His help in overcoming them. By addressing these hidden sins and habits, we experience a sense of freedom and peace, knowing that we are living in a way that honors God and reflects His character.

The process of letting Scripture search our hearts also involves discovering our true desires and passions. God has placed unique dreams, talents, and passions within each of us, but sometimes these can become buried under the busyness of life, the expectations of others, or our own insecurities. When we spend time in God's Word, it helps us reconnect with these desires, reminding us of the purpose and calling that God has for our lives. A verse about serving others might awaken a passion for helping those in need, or a passage about using our gifts for God's glory might inspire us to pursue a talent we've neglected. By revealing these desires, the Bible encourages us to live boldly and fully for God, using the gifts He's given us to make a positive impact on the world. This clarity of purpose brings a sense of fulfillment and joy, as we align our lives with the passions and dreams that God has placed within our hearts.

Another way that God's Word searches our hearts is by helping us recognize and confront our fears and insecurities. Often, we may hold onto fears about the future, doubts about our worth, or worries about our abilities, and these can keep us from fully trusting in God or stepping out in faith. The Bible addresses these fears by reminding us of God's promises, His love, and His faithfulness. When we come across verses that speak of God's protection, provision, and guidance, they act like a balm to our fears, calming our anxieties and giving us the courage to trust in Him. By revealing these fears and insecurities, Scripture helps us bring them to God, allowing His peace and strength to fill our hearts. This trust in God replaces fear with confidence, empowering us to move forward with faith and hope, knowing that we are never alone and that God is always with us.

Scripture also searches our hearts by challenging us to grow in love, compassion, and empathy for others. The Bible is filled with teachings about loving our neighbors, forgiving those who hurt us, and showing kindness to everyone we meet. These teachings encourage us to look beyond ourselves and to consider how we treat those around us. Sometimes, we may realize that we've been quick to judge, slow to forgive, or indifferent to others' struggles. By exposing these areas, God's Word challenges us to grow in love and to treat others with the same grace and compassion that we've received from Him. This growth in love not only strengthens our relationships but also helps us to become more Christ-like, reflecting His love to a world that desperately needs it.

Ultimately, the process of allowing God's Word to search our hearts brings us closer to Him. As we become more aware of our thoughts, intentions, and hidden aspects, we gain a deeper understanding of who we are in God's eyes and who He is calling us to be. This awareness leads us to seek God's guidance more earnestly, to rely on His strength more fully, and to embrace His grace more deeply. By letting Scripture reveal areas where we need growth or change, we are continually drawn back to God, allowing Him to shape us, mold us, and transform us into people who reflect His love, truth, and grace in every part of our lives.

Chapter 20 - Soul-Healing

The concept of Soul-Healing through God's Word is one of the most powerful ways that the Bible transforms lives because it speaks directly to the deep, often hidden wounds and brokenness within us. Life can leave us with emotional scars, whether from loss, disappointment, rejection, betrayal, or personal failures. These wounds can be so deep that they shape the way we see ourselves, others, and even God. They may linger, affecting our hearts, thoughts, and actions in ways we might not fully understand. But God's Word has the unique ability to "divide soul and spirit," reaching into those hidden places where our hurt resides, and bringing healing that no human words, advice, or medicine can offer. Unlike anything else, Scripture speaks with a divine wisdom and love that soothes our hearts and minds, giving comfort and hope even in the darkest and most painful areas of our lives. When we spend time in the Bible, we're not just reading words on a page; we're engaging with the living Word of God that can address our deepest needs. The Bible offers promises of God's love, reminders of His forgiveness, and reassurances of His presence, all of which speak to our pain and invite us to experience healing on a profound level. This soul-healing process is gradual and gentle, as God meets us where we are, helping us to release our burdens, let go of bitterness, and find peace in His grace and compassion. Spending time in Scripture becomes a refuge, a place where we can be honest about our hurt and find the strength to move forward with a healed and renewed heart.

One of the most amazing things about the healing power of God's Word is that it doesn't just mask the pain; it addresses it at its core, allowing true healing to take place. Sometimes, when we're hurting, we might try to ignore the pain, distract ourselves, or push it down, hoping it will eventually go away. But unresolved pain can grow, leading to feelings of anger, sadness, or even self-doubt. The Bible, however, doesn't just cover up these feelings; it helps us confront them with God's truth and love. For instance, verses about God's forgiveness remind us that we are not defined by our mistakes and that we can release feelings of guilt or shame. Similarly, passages about God's unfailing love reassure us that we are never alone, even when we feel rejected or unloved by others. This truth allows us to let go of the past and start fresh, knowing that God is there to help us through every step of the healing process. As we meditate on these verses, they begin to sink into our hearts, slowly transforming our perspective and bringing us a sense of freedom and relief that only God's love can provide.

The Bible also speaks to the importance of forgiveness as part of the healing process. Often, our deepest wounds come from being hurt by others, and these can be hard to let go of. Holding onto grudges or resentment can weigh heavily on our hearts, keeping us trapped in pain. But God's Word teaches us about the power of forgiveness, not only for the person who wronged us but for our own well-being. When we read verses that encourage us to forgive, like "Forgive as the Lord forgave you," we realize that forgiveness is a gift we give to ourselves as well. By letting go of bitterness, we free ourselves from the control of the past and open our hearts to experience God's peace. This doesn't mean forgetting the pain or pretending it didn't happen; it means choosing to move forward, trusting that God will bring justice and healing in His way and timing. Forgiveness is a journey, and the Bible gives us the courage and strength to take those first steps, knowing that God's grace is sufficient to help us release what we cannot carry alone.

Another incredible aspect of soul-healing through Scripture is that it helps us rebuild our sense of worth and identity. Pain and rejection can sometimes make us question our value, leading us to feel unworthy or unloved. But the Bible constantly reminds us of our worth in God's eyes, telling us that we are "fearfully and wonderfully made" and that we are His beloved children. These truths help us reclaim our identity, seeing ourselves as God sees us rather than through the lens of our pain. By meditating on verses about God's love and purpose for us, we start to heal from feelings of inadequacy, insecurity, or shame. This renewed sense of identity is powerful, as it helps us walk in confidence and hope, knowing that we are cherished by a God who loves us unconditionally. This knowledge empowers us to face each day with a sense of dignity and strength, even if we've been hurt or rejected in the past.

Spending time in God's Word also provides comfort and hope, especially during times of grief or loss. When we lose someone or something important to us, it's natural to feel a deep sense of sadness, and healing can seem distant or impossible. But the Bible offers words of hope and encouragement, reminding us that God is close to the brokenhearted and that He understands our pain. Passages like Psalm 34:18, which says, "The Lord is close to the brokenhearted and saves those who are crushed in spirit," bring comfort in knowing that we are not alone in our sorrow. These verses remind us that God sees our tears and is present with us in our grief, holding us and offering a peace that surpasses understanding. This comfort doesn't take away the pain, but it gives us the strength to endure and the hope that healing is possible. By focusing on God's promises, we find a source of peace that helps us to keep moving forward, one day at a time.

Scripture also helps us heal by teaching us to trust God's plan for our lives, even when we don't understand why certain things happened. Life can bring unexpected challenges that leave us feeling lost or broken, and it's easy to wonder why God would allow us to go through such pain. But the Bible reassures us that God has a purpose for everything, even if we can't see it yet. Verses like Jeremiah 29:11, which says, "For I know the plans I have for you, declares the Lord, plans to prosper you and not to harm you, plans to give you hope and a future," remind us that God is always working for our good, even in the hardest times. This trust in God's sovereignty allows us to let go of trying to control or understand everything, freeing us to rest in His care. By believing in God's plan, we begin to see our pain as part of a bigger picture, one that He will ultimately use for His glory and our growth. This perspective brings a sense of peace and purpose to our lives, helping us to heal as we trust that God is guiding us, even through the valleys.

Healing through Scripture also brings a renewed sense of joy and hope, as we learn to focus on God's goodness and His promises for the future. The Bible is filled with messages of hope, reminding us that pain and suffering are not the end of our story. Verses like Romans 8:28, which says, "And we know that in all things God works for the good of those who love him," help us to see that God can bring beauty from our brokenness. This hope renews our spirit, filling us with joy that goes beyond our circumstances. It's a joy rooted in the knowledge that God is with us, that He has a plan, and that He is constantly working to heal, restore, and bless us. This joy becomes a source of strength, helping us to face each day with optimism and a positive outlook, even if we're still in the process of healing.

Ultimately, the healing that comes from God's Word transforms us from the inside out, allowing us to live with peace, purpose, and resilience. By spending time in Scripture, we invite God to work in our hearts, addressing our pain, guiding us toward forgiveness, and reminding us of our worth and His love. This healing is not always immediate; it is a journey that requires patience and faith. But with each verse we meditate on, each promise we hold onto, and each truth we apply, we move closer to a place of wholeness. God's Word is like medicine for the soul, providing exactly what we need to heal and grow, no matter how deep the wound or how long the journey. Through the healing power of Scripture, we find the strength to let go of the past, embrace the present, and look forward to the future with hope and confidence, knowing that God's love is leading us every step of the way.

Chapter 21 - Secures Eternity

The idea that God's Word Secures Eternity is one of the most powerful and comforting truths in Scripture, as it provides us with a deep assurance of salvation and the promise of eternal life. This assurance isn't just a vague hope or wish; it's a solid, unchanging promise from God Himself, given to us through the Bible. The Bible isn't just a collection of teachings for this life alone—it's a message from God that points us toward a future that goes beyond anything we could imagine. Through its pages, we learn about God's love, His plan for redemption, and His desire for us to be with Him forever. By believing in and accepting the truths found in Scripture, we are offered the incredible gift of eternal life, a life that is full of peace, joy, and unbroken fellowship with God. The Bible explains this pathway to eternal life with clarity, laying out God's plan from the beginning, showing us that Jesus Christ came to earth to pay the price for our sins so that we could be reconciled to God and secure an eternity with Him. This isn't something we can earn by being good or trying hard; it's a gift freely given by God's grace, available to anyone who believes. This promise of eternity changes the way we live now because it provides a sense of security, peace, and purpose that no earthly success or possession can give. When we accept God's Word as the ultimate truth, we know that our future is held firmly in His hands, and we can rest in the certainty that our lives are headed toward a glorious eternity with Him.

This assurance of salvation and eternal life provides an anchor for our souls, giving us peace in a world that is often full of uncertainty. Life on earth can be difficult, and we all experience moments of doubt, fear, and loss. But the Bible assures us that, through faith in Christ, we are secure in God's love and destined for a future that no earthly trouble can take away. Verses like John 3:16, which tells us that "God so loved the world that he gave his only Son, that whoever believes in him shall not perish but have eternal life," fill us with hope and peace, knowing that our eternity is guaranteed by the one who created us. This promise is a source of comfort when we face difficult times or when we wonder about the meaning of life and what comes next. Instead of living in fear or anxiety about the unknown, we can trust that God has already prepared a place for us, a place where there will be no more pain, no more tears, and no more death. This hope for eternity brings us joy and a steady peace that allows us to face whatever challenges come our way, knowing that our future is safe in God's hands.

The power of Scripture to secure eternity is rooted in the life, death, and resurrection of Jesus Christ. Throughout the Bible, we see God's plan for salvation unfold, showing us that Jesus' sacrifice on the cross paid the penalty for our sins, making a way for us to be forgiven and restored to God. This incredible act of love and grace is at the heart of our eternal security. Because Jesus overcame death, we too can have confidence that death is not the end for us. Instead, it is the doorway to a new life with God forever. When we place our trust in Jesus and follow the teachings of Scripture, we are promised a place in heaven, where we will experience the fullness of God's presence and love. This promise of eternity with God is not just a nice idea; it's the very foundation of our faith. It gives us hope beyond this life, reminding us that we are part of a larger story, one that began with God's creation of the world and will continue forever in His presence. This assurance gives us strength and courage, knowing that no matter what happens in this life, our eternity is secure because of what Jesus has done for us.

Scripture's promise of eternal life also gives us a sense of purpose and direction. Knowing that we are destined for eternity with God motivates us to live our lives in a way that honors Him and reflects His love to others. This eternal perspective helps us to focus on what truly matters, guiding us to invest our time, energy, and resources in things that have lasting value. Instead of getting caught up in the temporary concerns of this world, we can live with a greater purpose, knowing that our choices impact not only our lives but also our eternity and the eternity of others. This eternal outlook encourages us to share the hope of the gospel with those around us, helping them to find the same peace and security that we have. By living with our hearts focused on eternity, we experience a joy and fulfillment that comes from knowing we are part of God's eternal plan. This purpose is deeply satisfying, as it reminds us that our lives are meaningful and that everything we do for God has eternal significance.

The Bible also teaches us that eternal life is not just something we look forward to after we die; it begins now as we walk with God each day. Jesus said in John 17:3, "Now this is eternal life: that they know you, the only true God, and Jesus Christ, whom you have sent." This verse reminds us that eternal life is about having a relationship with God, knowing Him deeply and experiencing His love, peace, and presence in our lives now. As we grow in our relationship with God through studying His Word, praying, and living out our faith, we begin to experience a taste of eternity here on earth. This relationship with God fills us with a peace and joy that transcends circumstances, reminding us that no matter what we face, we are already living in the security of God's love and promises. This ongoing relationship with God is a glimpse of the eternal life we will fully experience in heaven, and it makes our daily lives richer and more meaningful.

The assurance of eternal life also brings us comfort when we lose loved ones who have put their faith in Christ. In times of grief, it is natural to feel sorrow and loss, but the promise of eternity gives us hope that we will see them again. Verses like 1 Thessalonians 4:13-14, which tell us not to "grieve like the rest of mankind, who have no hope," remind us that death is not the end for believers. This hope allows us to grieve with peace, knowing that our loved ones are with God and that we will be reunited with them one day. The assurance of eternity takes away the finality of death, replacing it with a confident expectation of life beyond this world. This hope brings healing and comfort, helping us to find strength in the midst of sorrow and to look forward to the day when all believers will be together in God's presence.

The Bible's promise of eternal life is also a reminder of God's love and faithfulness. Throughout Scripture, we see God's commitment to His people, His desire to save us, and His promise to be with us forever. This assurance of eternal life is a testament to God's unchanging love and His dedication to fulfilling His promises. When we read verses about eternal life, we are reminded that God is faithful and that His Word can be trusted. This knowledge strengthens our faith, helping us to rely on God's promises with confidence and to live with a sense of security, knowing that our future is in His hands. God's promise of eternal life is an expression of His desire for a relationship with us, one that will never end. This love gives us a sense of belonging and identity, knowing that we are part of God's family and that our lives have eternal significance.

Living with the security of eternity also changes the way we handle challenges and difficulties. When we know that our ultimate destiny is with God, we are better able to endure hardships with patience and hope. Life's trials become opportunities to grow in faith, knowing that these struggles are temporary compared to the eternal glory that awaits us. Verses like Romans 8:18, which says, "I consider that our present sufferings are not worth comparing with the glory that will be revealed in us," remind us to focus on the bigger picture. This eternal perspective helps us to remain hopeful and resilient, even when life is difficult, because we know that God has promised us a future beyond our current struggles. The security of eternity gives us a reason to persevere, knowing that every challenge brings us one step closer to the joy and peace of eternal life with God.

In conclusion, the assurance of eternity found in God's Word is one of the most precious gifts we have as believers. It provides a foundation of hope, peace, and purpose that transforms the way we live. By embracing the promise of eternal life, we find the strength to face life's challenges, the motivation to live with purpose, and the joy of knowing that our future is secure in God's hands. This promise changes everything, filling us with a peace that surpasses understanding and a confidence that comes from knowing we are loved and destined to be with God forever. Through Scripture, we can find true security, resting in the knowledge that eternity is ours through faith in Jesus Christ.

Chapter 22 - Source of Wisdom

The Bible as a Source of Wisdom is one of the most valuable aspects of Scripture because it provides us with divine guidance and understanding that are timeless, relevant, and applicable to every aspect of our lives. God's Word is not just a book of stories or ancient teachings; it's filled with wisdom that speaks to our hearts and minds, giving us insight into how to live a life that is grounded in truth, love, and purpose. This wisdom is special because it doesn't change with the trends or shifting opinions of society—it is constant and reliable, coming directly from God, who knows all things and sees the full picture of our lives and the world around us. When we turn to Scripture, we find answers to life's big questions as well as guidance for the small, everyday decisions that shape who we are. The Bible offers advice on relationships, finances, forgiveness, handling stress, facing fear, and so much more, providing principles that we can apply to any situation. This divine wisdom helps us avoid common pitfalls, make choices that bring peace and fulfillment, and live a life that honors God. Whether we're facing a challenging decision, looking for direction, or simply seeking to grow in character, the Bible has something to say to guide us in the right direction.

One of the reasons the Bible's wisdom is so powerful is that it connects us to God's heart and perspective. Unlike human wisdom, which is often limited by personal experience or cultural influence, God's wisdom is perfect, covering all aspects of life from an eternal viewpoint. In Proverbs 3:5-6, we're told to "trust in the Lord with all your heart and lean not on your own understanding; in all your ways submit to him, and he will make your paths straight." This verse reminds us that our own understanding is limited, but God's guidance is trustworthy and true. When we rely on Scripture, we are choosing to trust in God's perspective, which goes beyond what we can see or understand. This gives us the courage to make decisions with faith, knowing that God's wisdom will lead us toward what is truly good and beneficial, even if it's not immediately clear to us. Each time we turn to the Bible for wisdom, we're choosing to align our lives with God's perfect will, allowing Him to guide us with insight and understanding that are far greater than our own.

Scripture is filled with practical wisdom that applies to real-life situations, helping us navigate relationships, challenges, and personal growth. For example, the Bible teaches us the value of kindness, honesty, humility, and patience—all qualities that improve our interactions with others and contribute to healthier relationships. When we follow biblical principles, we're less likely to fall into conflicts fueled by pride, jealousy, or anger. Instead, we're encouraged to approach others with love, respect, and understanding. This wisdom also helps us in our relationships with family, friends, and coworkers, showing us how to communicate effectively, resolve disagreements peacefully, and offer forgiveness freely. These teachings create a foundation for strong, loving connections that bring joy and support to our lives. By following the Bible's guidance in our relationships, we create an atmosphere of harmony and respect, reflecting God's love in the way we treat others. This wisdom from Scripture enriches our lives and strengthens our communities, helping us to live with integrity and kindness.

The Bible's wisdom also extends to our personal growth and character development. Throughout Scripture, we're encouraged to grow in qualities like patience, self-control, humility, and generosity. These traits are not only beneficial for our spiritual lives but also for our overall well-being. When we practice patience, we're less likely to make impulsive decisions that we might later regret. When we embrace humility, we're open to learning from others and becoming better versions of ourselves. By practicing self-control, we're able to make choices that lead to healthier and more fulfilling lives, free from the control of negative habits or destructive behaviors. The Bible's wisdom doesn't just tell us what to avoid; it shows us how to build a life filled with positive, godly qualities that make us more compassionate, resilient, and joyful. This growth in character helps us to reflect God's goodness in our actions and to inspire others to seek the same wisdom that has guided and blessed our lives.

In times of difficulty or uncertainty, the Bible offers wisdom that brings comfort and peace. Life is full of challenges—loss, disappointment, stress, and fear—and it's easy to feel overwhelmed or uncertain about what to do. But

Scripture provides reassurance and guidance, reminding us that God is with us and that we can trust Him even when things seem unclear. Verses like Philippians 4:6-7, which encourage us to "not be anxious about anything, but in every situation, by prayer and petition, with thanksgiving, present your requests to God," teach us to bring our worries to God and to rely on His peace. This wisdom helps us to handle life's challenges with faith and calmness, knowing that God is in control and that He cares for us deeply. By turning to Scripture in difficult times, we find a source of strength that lifts our spirits and gives us the courage to face each day with hope. This peace and reassurance are part of the Bible's wisdom, providing us with a steady foundation that keeps us grounded, even when life feels unstable.

The wisdom in the Bible also guides us in managing our resources, such as time, money, and talents, in a way that honors God. Proverbs, for instance, offers numerous insights on handling finances wisely, avoiding debt, and being generous to those in need. These teachings remind us that everything we have is a gift from God, and we are called to use it responsibly. By applying these principles, we're able to avoid financial stress, live within our means, and share with others. Additionally, the Bible encourages us to use our time wisely, focusing on things that bring us closer to God and allow us to serve others. This wisdom helps us to prioritize what truly matters, avoiding distractions that pull us away from our purpose. By managing our resources according to God's guidance, we find a sense of satisfaction and balance that enriches our lives and allows us to bless those around us.

Turning to the Bible for wisdom also gives us insight into God's purpose for our lives. Many people search for meaning and direction, wondering what they are meant to do and why they are here. Scripture answers these questions by reminding us that we are created by God, with unique gifts and talents, for a specific purpose. Jeremiah 29:11 assures us that God has plans for us—plans to prosper us and not to harm us, plans to give us hope and a future. This wisdom encourages us to seek God's will, to trust His guidance, and to pursue a life that aligns with His purpose. Knowing that our lives have meaning and that God has a plan for each of us gives us motivation and joy, helping us to live each day with a sense of purpose and fulfillment. This guidance brings clarity to our goals and ambitions, reminding us that true success is found in following God's will and using our lives to glorify Him.

The Bible's wisdom also helps us to make ethical and moral decisions, providing a standard of right and wrong that we can trust. In a world where values and morals can often feel relative or uncertain, Scripture gives us a clear foundation for understanding what is truly good, just, and loving. The Ten Commandments, for example, offer timeless principles for living a life that honors God and respects others. By following these guidelines, we avoid the pitfalls of dishonesty, greed, and selfishness, choosing instead to live with integrity, honesty, and compassion. This moral wisdom is not about following rules for the sake of rules; it's about living in a way that brings peace, respect, and harmony to our lives and to our communities. By aligning our actions with God's standards, we find a sense of peace and purpose that goes beyond what the world can offer, knowing that we are living in a way that pleases God.

Finally, the wisdom found in the Bible is timeless, relevant for every generation and every culture. No matter how the world changes, God's principles remain true and effective, guiding people through all types of situations and challenges. This timeless nature of Scripture shows us that God's wisdom is not limited by time or place—it is universal, offering guidance that applies to everyone, everywhere. This universality makes the Bible a source of wisdom that we can trust completely, knowing that it has guided countless others before us and will continue to guide generations to come. By turning to the Bible for wisdom, we are joining a legacy of believers who have found hope, peace, and purpose through God's Word. This wisdom is a precious gift that enriches our lives, helping us to grow in faith, character, and understanding. In every area of life, from our relationships to our choices, from our work to our faith, the Bible provides the wisdom we need to live fully and faithfully as God intended.

Chapter 23 - Strength Against Temptation

The Strength Against Temptation that comes from God's Word is one of the most powerful tools we have in our spiritual journey, as it provides us with the power to cut through deception and resist sin. Temptation is a universal challenge—everyone faces it in different forms, whether it's the temptation to act out of anger, to give in to jealousy, to lie, to indulge in harmful behaviors, or to pursue selfish desires. These temptations can pull us away from what we know is right, and without something strong to hold onto, it's easy to be led astray. However, God's Word gives us the strength and clarity we need to stand firm in the face of these temptations. The Bible is described as being sharper than any two-edged sword, meaning it can slice through the lies and justifications that temptations often come with, exposing them for what they really are—harmful paths that lead us away from God's best for us. By memorizing Scripture, we're able to call upon God's truth in moments when we feel weak or unsure. When Jesus was tempted in the wilderness, He responded to every temptation with Scripture, saying, "It is written…" each time the devil tried to deceive Him (Matthew 4:1-11). Jesus' example shows us the incredible power of knowing and speaking God's Word in moments of temptation. Each verse we memorize becomes a weapon, giving us the strength to reject lies, overcome urges, and choose what honors God, even when it's difficult. This practice doesn't just build our willpower; it builds our faith, anchoring us in God's truth and helping us to live with integrity, no matter what challenges come our way.

One of the most amazing aspects of using Scripture to resist temptation is that it doesn't just help us avoid sin—it helps us grow closer to God. When we choose to stand on His Word instead of giving in to our own desires, we're showing trust in His wisdom and love. This trust strengthens our relationship with God, filling us with peace and satisfaction that goes far beyond the temporary pleasures of sin. Every time we turn to the Bible for strength, we're drawing closer to God, allowing His truth to shape our thoughts and guide our actions. This deepens our understanding of His character, helping us to see that His commands are not just rules to follow but are actually for our benefit. God's Word isn't meant to limit us; it's meant to protect us from harm and to lead us toward a life of joy, peace, and purpose. By memorizing verses that address specific areas of struggle, we're able to find the specific encouragement and wisdom we need in our moments of weakness, making it easier to choose what honors God rather than what may seem appealing in the moment. This is how Scripture not only prevents us from falling into temptation but also transforms our hearts, filling us with a love for God's ways that makes resisting sin feel less like a struggle and more like a joy.

Scripture provides strength against temptation by reminding us of God's promises and helping us focus on the bigger picture. Temptation often tries to lure us in by making us think only about the immediate pleasure or relief we might feel, ignoring the long-term consequences or the way it affects our relationship with God. But the Bible helps us keep our eyes on what truly matters, reminding us that choosing God's way is always worth it, even if it's hard at first. Verses like James 1:12, which says, "Blessed is the one who perseveres under trial because, having stood the test, that person will receive the crown of life that the Lord has promised to those who love him," give us the motivation to stand firm. This promise of reward and eternal life helps us to see that resisting temptation is not just about saying "no" to something harmful; it's about saying "yes" to a closer walk with God, a life of purpose, and the joy of knowing we are pleasing Him. Each time we choose to resist, we're training ourselves to value God's promises over fleeting pleasures, building a character that is rooted in faith and strengthened by God's Word.

The Bible also provides practical wisdom for avoiding situations that may lead us into temptation. By studying Scripture, we learn to recognize our weaknesses and understand the kinds of situations that might make us more vulnerable to sin. For instance, verses that talk about guarding our hearts or being cautious about our associations remind us to be mindful of the influences around us and the choices we make each day. Proverbs 4:23 says, "Above all else, guard your heart, for everything you do flows from it." This wisdom encourages us to create boundaries that protect us from stumbling, like choosing friends who encourage us to make good choices, avoiding environments that trigger negative behaviors, and focusing on activities that build us up rather than pull us down. The Bible helps us to see that resisting temptation isn't just about fighting in the moment; it's also about setting ourselves up for success by staying close to God and keeping our minds focused on His truth. This guidance makes it easier to walk in integrity and to make decisions that honor God, building a life that reflects His love and wisdom.

Another powerful way Scripture strengthens us against temptation is by filling us with the Holy Spirit's power. As we spend time in God's Word, we invite the Holy Spirit to work in us, giving us strength, wisdom, and self-control. Galatians 5:16 says, "So I say, walk by the Spirit, and you will not gratify the desires of the flesh." When we rely on the Spirit, we're no longer trying to resist temptation in our own strength but are empowered by God's presence within us. This partnership with the Holy Spirit gives us a sense of peace and assurance, knowing that we're not alone in our struggles. The Spirit brings verses to mind when we need them most, strengthens our resolve, and helps us to focus on God's love and guidance instead of the pull of temptation. This inner strength makes us more resilient, able to face even the strongest urges or pressures with a calm and confident heart. By staying close to God through Scripture, we experience the Spirit's power in a way that transforms our lives, making us more like Christ in our thoughts, actions, and choices.

Memorizing Scripture as a defense against temptation also builds a foundation of truth in our minds, helping us to resist lies or half-truths that might lead us astray. Temptation often comes with subtle deceptions, convincing us that something wrong is actually okay, that nobody will know, or that it doesn't really matter. But when we know God's Word, we're able to recognize these lies immediately, responding with the truth that God has shown us. For example, when we're tempted to think that our actions don't matter, verses that remind us of our purpose and calling as God's children give us the clarity to choose what honors Him. By filling our minds with Scripture, we create a mental and spiritual "armor" that protects us from false ideas and keeps us rooted in what is right. This foundation of truth allows us to see temptation for what it really is—a distraction from God's best for us—and gives us the confidence to say "no" with conviction.

The Bible's strength against temptation also lies in the hope it offers for a life of freedom and joy. God's Word assures us that we don't have to be controlled by our desires or weaknesses; we can experience true freedom by walking in His ways. Romans 6:18 says, "You have been set free from sin and have become slaves to righteousness." This freedom means that we're no longer bound to the things that used to hold us back. Each time we turn to Scripture in moments of temptation, we're reminded that God has given us the power to overcome, to rise above our struggles, and to live a life that is filled with His peace and joy. This promise of freedom motivates us to keep resisting, knowing that each choice to follow God brings us closer to the abundant life He has planned for us.

Ultimately, God's Word as a source of strength against temptation is about more than just avoiding sin—it's about building a life that is centered on God's love and truth. By memorizing Scripture, we are equipping ourselves with the tools we need to live with integrity, courage, and faith, no matter what challenges come our way. This commitment to knowing and applying God's Word transforms our hearts, making us more like Christ and filling our lives with a sense of purpose and joy that nothing else can offer. Each time we choose God's way over temptation, we are growing stronger in faith, becoming more rooted in His love, and experiencing the true freedom that comes from walking in obedience to His Word.

Chapter 24 - Softens Hearts

The Softening of Hearts through God's Word is one of the most transformative effects of Scripture, as it has the unique ability to pierce deeply, reaching and reshaping even the hardest of hearts. Life experiences, disappointments, and wounds can sometimes make our hearts hard and closed off, building walls of resistance, bitterness, or indifference. This hardening can make us resistant to love, forgiveness, and the peace God wants us to experience. However, God's Word is powerful, able to cut through these barriers and reach the core of who we are, where His truth and love can work to soften and transform us. The Bible describes itself as sharper than any two-edged sword, capable of dividing soul and spirit, and this imagery shows us that it is not just a book of comforting words but a powerful tool that God uses to break through the hard layers around our hearts. When we open ourselves to Scripture, we allow God to work in us, gently breaking down those defenses that have kept us from experiencing His love fully. This softening isn't a quick or easy process, but as we regularly spend time in God's Word, it starts to change us from the inside out, making our hearts more receptive to His voice, His love, and His guidance. It's as if each verse we read acts like a gentle drop of water on stone, slowly wearing down the hardness and creating a heart that is soft, open, and willing to receive God's truth.

One of the most remarkable things about how Scripture softens our hearts is that it does so with both truth and grace. The Bible doesn't shy away from confronting us with hard truths about our thoughts, attitudes, and actions, but it always does so with love, offering us a better way. For instance, we may come across verses that challenge us to forgive, even when it feels impossible, or verses that encourage humility when pride is deeply ingrained in us. These teachings confront us, showing us areas where we might be resisting God's will, but they also show us the beauty of living in line with God's character. Each truth, even if difficult to accept at first, is accompanied by the assurance of God's love and the promise of a life filled with peace, joy, and purpose when we follow His ways. This balance of truth and grace helps to soften our hearts in a way that is gentle yet effective, leading us to willingly surrender the hardness we may have held onto. Through Scripture, God calls us to let go of bitterness, anger, fear, and anything else that might keep us from Him, not with harsh demands, but with a loving invitation to experience something better—His peace and His presence.

The process of softening our hearts through Scripture also helps us to grow in compassion and empathy for others. A hardened heart often focuses on self-preservation, building walls to avoid pain or vulnerability, which can make us less sensitive to the needs and feelings of those around us. But as we spend time in God's Word, reading about His love for all people and His call for us to love one another, our perspective begins to shift. Verses that encourage kindness, patience, and forgiveness start to resonate deeply within us, prompting us to reach out with love rather than judgment. This shift makes us more aware of others' struggles and more willing to show grace, even when it's challenging. By softening our hearts, Scripture transforms the way we see and treat others, helping us to become vessels of God's love and kindness in a world that often lacks both. This transformation doesn't happen overnight, but with each passage we reflect on, our hearts become a little softer, a little more open to loving as God loves.

Another powerful effect of Scripture's softening work is the healing it brings to old wounds and past hurts. Often, a hardened heart is a result of unresolved pain or disappointment that has left scars on our spirit. These hurts can make us wary of trusting others or even of trusting God fully, as we may fear being hurt again. But the Bible offers healing words that gently mend these broken areas, reminding us of God's constant love and His ability to turn even painful experiences into sources of growth and strength. Verses about God's comfort, His healing, and His presence in our suffering help to ease the pain and bring a sense of peace that softens the anger, fear, or sadness we might have been holding onto. This healing process allows us to let go of the burdens we've carried, freeing us to embrace life with a heart that is open to love, joy, and new possibilities. Through Scripture, we're reminded that God sees our pain and wants to heal it, that we are not alone, and that we can trust Him to carry us through any trial. This trust in God's goodness and care gradually melts away the hardness that pain has created, opening our hearts to receive His love more fully.

Scripture also softens our hearts by teaching us humility. A hardened heart often resists correction or refuses to admit faults, driven by pride or the fear of appearing weak. But as we read God's Word, we're reminded that humility is a virtue, a strength rather than a weakness. Verses that call us to put others first, to be patient, and to seek wisdom from God rather than relying solely on our own understanding help us to see the value of a humble heart. This humility doesn't make us feel small or insignificant; rather, it opens us to God's greatness and His ability to work through us in ways we could never accomplish on our own. By embracing humility, we allow God to shape us, to correct us, and to lead us toward a life that reflects His love and wisdom. This acceptance of our need for God softens our hearts, making us receptive to His guidance and willing to grow in ways that bring us closer to Him.

The Bible's role in softening our hearts also allows us to experience deeper gratitude and joy. A hardened heart often focuses on what's lacking, what's unfair, or what has gone wrong, which can lead to bitterness and dissatisfaction. But when we immerse ourselves in Scripture, we're reminded of God's countless blessings, His faithfulness, and His presence in our lives. Verses that encourage thankfulness, even in difficult times, help us to see the beauty of God's work in every situation, fostering a sense of gratitude that fills our hearts with joy. This gratitude shifts our focus from what we don't have to what God has given us, from our struggles to His promises. As we cultivate a heart of thankfulness, the hardness of resentment and discontent begins to dissolve, replaced by a peace and joy that come from recognizing God's goodness in every part of our lives. This joy is not based on circumstances but on the assurance of God's love, which softens our hearts and fills us with a sense of fulfillment that can't be shaken.

Ultimately, the softening of our hearts through Scripture prepares us to be more responsive to God's will and to the leading of the Holy Spirit. A soft heart is one that is open, willing to listen, and eager to follow where God leads, even if it requires stepping out of our comfort zone. By breaking down the walls of resistance, pride, and fear, the Bible makes us more sensitive to God's voice, helping us to recognize His guidance and to act with courage and faith. This readiness to follow God's will brings a sense of purpose and direction to our lives, as we learn to trust Him more fully and to walk in obedience to His calling. Each time we respond to God's Word with a willing heart, we're taking steps toward a life that is fully aligned with His purpose, filled with peace, joy, and a sense of fulfillment that only comes from following God's plan. This openness to God's will is the ultimate sign of a softened heart, one that is free from the burdens of bitterness, fear, and pride, and fully devoted to living out God's love and truth in every aspect of life.

Through the softening power of Scripture, we become more than just believers; we become transformed, living reflections of God's love and grace. This transformation is a lifelong journey, but with each verse we read, each truth we embrace, and each step of faith we take, our hearts become more like Christ's—filled with compassion, humility, joy, and a deep desire to serve God and others. This is the incredible power of God's Word to soften and renew us, creating hearts that are open to His love and eager to share it with the world.

Chapter 25 - Sustains Hope

The ability of God's Word to Sustain Hope is one of its most powerful qualities, as it provides a constant source of encouragement, strength, and peace, especially in times of struggle. The Bible is not just a collection of ancient writings; it is powerful and alive, speaking directly to our hearts and minds, reminding us that no matter what we're going through, there is always hope. Life can be incredibly challenging, filled with moments of pain, loss, uncertainty, and fear, and it's easy to feel overwhelmed or discouraged when things don't go as planned. But the promises in Scripture offer a foundation that we can stand on, even when everything around us seems to be falling apart. God's Word gives us hope that is unshakeable because it is based on His character—His goodness, faithfulness, and love. This hope is not just a fleeting feeling; it's a confident expectation that God is with us, that He has a purpose for our lives, and that He is working everything for our good. By resting in the promises found in Scripture, we are reminded that God sees us, hears us, and cares deeply about our struggles. Verses like Jeremiah 29:11, which tell us that God has "plans to prosper you and not to harm you, plans to give you hope and a future," fill us with a sense of purpose and assurance, knowing that our lives are held in God's hands. This enduring hope gives us the courage to keep going, even when we don't have all the answers or when life feels heavy. Each time we turn to the Bible, we find new reminders of God's love and faithfulness, which lift our spirits and renew our strength, allowing us to face each day with a heart full of hope.

One of the reasons God's Word is such a powerful source of hope is that it provides us with perspective, helping us see beyond our current struggles to the bigger picture. The Bible reminds us that our lives are part of a greater story, one that began with creation and will continue into eternity. This eternal perspective helps us to see our challenges in a different light, recognizing that they are temporary compared to the joy and peace that await us in God's presence. When we read verses like Romans 8:18, which says, "I consider that our present sufferings are not worth comparing with the glory that will be revealed in us," we're reminded that our pain is not permanent and that something greater is coming. This hope-filled outlook helps us endure, knowing that God's promises are true and that He is faithful to fulfill them. By focusing on the promises of eternity, we find the strength to persevere through difficulties, with the assurance that there is purpose in our suffering and that God is working in ways we may not yet understand.

God's Word sustains hope by reminding us of His faithfulness throughout history. The Bible is filled with stories of people who faced incredible hardships yet experienced God's provision, guidance, and deliverance. From Moses leading the Israelites through the Red Sea to David facing Goliath, each story serves as a testimony to God's power and His commitment to His people. These accounts remind us that God has been faithful in the past and will continue to be faithful today. When we read about His miraculous works and His promises kept, our own faith and hope are strengthened, as we realize that the same God who helped them is with us now. This knowledge that God is unchanging and that He always fulfills His promises gives us a strong foundation to hold onto, no matter what trials we face. By connecting with these stories, we're reminded that we are not alone in our struggles and that we are part of a legacy of faith, surrounded by those who have trusted in God and found hope in Him.

Scripture also sustains hope by filling us with peace and assurance in God's love. One of the most comforting truths in the Bible is that God's love for us is constant and unbreakable. Verses like Romans 8:38-39, which remind us that "nothing can separate us from the love of God that is in Christ Jesus our Lord," provide a sense of security that nothing else can offer. This love gives us hope because it assures us that, no matter what we face, we are deeply cared for and that God will never abandon us. This assurance allows us to face our fears, to release our worries, and to rest in the knowledge that we are held by a love that is far greater than any obstacle or challenge. This love, which is unchanging and unconditional, fills our hearts with hope, reminding us that God is always with us, even in the darkest times. By resting in His love, we find the courage to face each day with confidence, knowing that we are not facing life's struggles alone.

Another way God's Word sustains hope is by teaching us to trust in His timing and His plans. Life doesn't always go the way we expect, and it's easy to feel discouraged or frustrated when things don't happen on our timeline. But the Bible reminds us that God's timing is perfect and that His ways are higher than ours. Verses like Isaiah 55:8-9, which say, "For my thoughts are not your thoughts, neither are your ways my ways," help us to surrender our plans to God and to trust that He knows what is best. This trust in God's timing brings hope, as it allows us to let go of control and to believe that, even if we can't see it yet, God is working all things together for our good. This patience and trust give us a steady hope, helping us to remain peaceful and confident, even when life feels uncertain or delayed. By focusing on God's promises rather than our own expectations, we learn to rest in His wisdom, finding hope in the knowledge that His plans are always for our ultimate good.

The Bible's hope-sustaining power also comes from its ability to renew our minds, filling us with positive and life-giving thoughts. In times of struggle, it's easy to fall into patterns of negative thinking, focusing on our fears, failures, or doubts. But Scripture provides a way to shift our focus, reminding us of God's promises and His power. Verses like Philippians 4:8 encourage us to think about "whatever is true, noble, right, pure, lovely, admirable," helping us to lift our thoughts above our worries and to find hope in God's truth. By meditating on these positive truths, we replace our fears with faith, our doubts with trust, and our worries with peace. This transformation of our minds renews our hope, as we're reminded of God's goodness, His control, and His love for us. This daily renewal keeps our hearts focused on hope, allowing us to face each challenge with a mindset that is grounded in God's promises rather than our own uncertainties.

The Bible also sustains hope by encouraging us to pray and seek God's presence. In times of difficulty, prayer becomes a powerful way to connect with God, to share our struggles, and to receive His comfort and guidance. Verses like 1 Thessalonians 5:17, which encourage us to "pray continually," remind us that we have constant access to God's presence and that we can bring our worries and fears to Him at any time. This ongoing connection with God through prayer keeps our hope alive, as it fills us with a sense of peace and security, knowing that He hears us and that He is actively involved in our lives. By making prayer a regular part of our lives, we're able to face challenges with hope, knowing that we have a direct line to the One who has all the answers and who holds our future in His hands.

Finally, Scripture sustains hope by pointing us to Jesus, the ultimate source of hope and salvation. Jesus' life, death, and resurrection are the foundation of our hope, as they remind us that God's love is stronger than sin, suffering, and even death itself. Verses like John 16:33, where Jesus says, "In this world you will have trouble. But take heart! I have overcome the world," remind us that, through Him, we have victory over anything that comes our way. This hope in Jesus gives us the strength to face our struggles with courage, knowing that our Savior has already won the ultimate battle. His resurrection assures us of eternal life, giving us a hope that goes beyond this world and its troubles. This hope in Christ is unbreakable, as it is rooted in the greatest act of love and power the world has ever seen. By focusing on Jesus and His promises, we find a hope that sustains us through every trial, filling our hearts with peace, joy, and an unshakable faith in God's goodness.

God's Word is a wellspring of hope, providing us with the encouragement, strength, and peace we need to face life's challenges with confidence. By resting in the promises of Scripture, we find a hope that is enduring and powerful, one that lifts us above our struggles and fills our hearts with a sense of purpose and assurance. This hope is a gift that transforms our lives, helping us to walk in faith and to trust in God's plan, knowing that our future is secure in His hands. Through God's Word, we discover a hope that sustains us, bringing light to even the darkest days and filling our hearts with a peace that only He can give.

Conclusion

The conclusion of "The Power and Precision of God's Word" reminds us that as Christians, we have been given an extraordinary gift in the Bible—a source of guidance, strength, wisdom, and encouragement that can sustain us throughout life's journey. This book has shown how Scripture is alive and active, able to cut through confusion, bring peace in struggles, and provide hope that lasts. Now, as we finish this exploration of God's Word, we are called not to leave it on the shelf or let these lessons fade but to continue walking with the Bible as our daily companion. The Word of God is meant to be alive in us, working within our hearts and minds to shape us into the people God calls us to be. This is not a one-time lesson; it's a lifelong journey. As Christians, we're encouraged to keep reading, studying, and meditating on Scripture, making it the foundation of our decisions, actions, and values. We've learned how God's Word pierces deeply to reach the hidden parts of our hearts, revealing what needs healing, growth, or change. We've seen how it strengthens our faith, helps us stand firm against temptation, and offers comfort when life feels overwhelming. This power of Scripture doesn't end with the closing of this book. It's a power that is meant to be revisited daily, to be applied to new situations, and to deepen our relationship with God every step of the way.

As we move forward, the Bible should be the light that guides us through both the easy and hard days. Just as a compass keeps travelers on course, God's Word is there to keep us grounded and moving in the right direction, aligned with His will. This means opening our Bibles regularly, letting the truths we've learned sink in deeper each time, and being willing to let God continue to work within us. The Christian journey isn't a straight line; it's filled with challenges, questions, and moments where faith is tested. But through it all, Scripture is there to reassure, to remind, and to strengthen. When doubts arise, when fear threatens to shake us, we can return to God's promises and find confidence in knowing that He is always faithful. Continuing in the Word also means sharing what we've learned with others, letting our lives be a reflection of the hope and truth that the Bible brings. This is a call to live boldly, to be a light in the world, and to invite others to experience the peace and power of God's Word for themselves.

As Christians, we're never meant to walk alone, and God's Word serves as a constant companion that teaches, corrects, and encourages us. The journey with Scripture is not about reaching perfection, but about ongoing growth and transformation, becoming more like Christ day by day. It's about letting the Word shape our responses to challenges, fill us with compassion, and inspire us to live with purpose and courage. The power and precision of God's Word is something we can rely on for the rest of our lives, knowing that each time we open the Bible, there is something new God wants to show us. The Christian life is a calling to remain rooted in this powerful truth, allowing it to transform us and to continually lead us closer to God. So, as we close this book, let us open our hearts even wider to the ongoing journey with Scripture, trusting that God will continue to speak, to guide, and to be our unshakeable foundation through every step of life.

Don't miss out!

Visit the website below and you can sign up to receive emails whenever Joshua Rhoades publishes a new book. There's no charge and no obligation.

https://books2read.com/r/B-A-AJLBB-VMQHF

BOOKS2READ

Connecting independent readers to independent writers.

Did you love *The Power and Precision of God's Word*? Then you should read *Answer The Call - 31 Days of Biblical Action*[1] by Joshua Rhoades!

[2]

"Answer the Call – 31 Days of Biblical Action" is a transformative devotional that challenges you to not only read the Word of God but to live it every day. This powerful 31-day guide is uniquely centered around individual action verbs drawn from Scripture, calling you to apply specific actions in your daily life. Each day highlights a verb—such as love, serve, forgive, trust, or pray—and encourages you to engage deeply with its biblical meaning while putting it into practice.

This is not just a devotional for reflection; it's a call to action, a stirring reminder that faith is most alive when it moves. By focusing on one verb each day, "Answer the Call" helps you to integrate the teachings of the Bible into your daily routine, bringing the message of Scripture to life in practical and meaningful ways.

---

1. https://books2read.com/u/4X5kG9

2. https://books2read.com/u/4X5kG9

The book invites you to engage your heart and hands as you follow Christ's example. Each action verb acts as a catalyst for spiritual growth, reminding you that faith isn't static but dynamic and responsive. Whether it's through acts of kindness, moments of prayer, or stepping out in faith, these daily challenges will inspire you to live out your beliefs with boldness and purpose.

By the end of the 31 days, you will feel encouraged, empowered, and renewed. "Answer the Call" will leave you transformed, ready to live your faith in real, actionable ways, embodying the teachings of Scripture in every area of your life.